Missus on a motorbike

Jackie Hartley

Highflyers Resources

The author

Jackie Hartley is a wife, mother, grandmother and all round busy lady. In her work life she helps students and graduates find jobs working as a Careers Adviser in her local university. She also, until recently, co-owned and ran a highly successful careers resources publishing company, through which she wrote and published a wide range of careers books and other materials. She wrote this book several years ago as a bit of light relief from her day job. Then she put it in a box on top of the wardrobe and forgot all about it. It came to light recently during a clear out and she decided to self publish it so that at least she would have something to give family members for Christmas. She lives in Stafford.

Please note, the motorbike riding tests and rider requirements may have changed since this book was written.

ISBN 13: 978-1-903449-48-6

Ⓐ Highflyers Resources Ltd
25 St Leonards Ave
Stafford
Staffordshire
ST17 4LT

Ⓣ 01785 257744

Ⓔ mike@highflyerspublishing.co.uk
Ⓦ www.highflyersresources.co.uk

For Harry, Louie, Kit and Maia.
May your lives also be full of adventures.

_____

Acknowledgements

This book is based on a true story and no names have been changed, so if you read it and recognise yourself, thank you for being a part of my life during that exciting time! The one person I really do have to thank, though, is Mike, my wonderful husband without whom this book and indeed my wonderful life as I know it, would not be possible. I just hope that, true to form, he doesn't bother to read this and get all full of himself. Thanks Mike, I love you.

Contents

Why would anyone want to ride a motorbike?

It's not that I'm afraid to die, I just don't want to be there when it happens.
Woody Allen

Driving to my new job, one sunny morning, I came across a scene of carnage. The car was half on the verge, half on the road. The bike was piled up on the central reservation and the rider was laid on the carriageway with his head propped up on the kerb. I stopped the car and dodged the traffic which just continued to flow off the roundabout, onto the dual carriageway and away. I remember running to the car first. The woman's face was sheet white and she was shaking badly, her hands locked to the steering wheel. She was muttering 'I'm sorry, I'm so sorry ..' I banged on the window. 'Are you okay?' The shaking got worse. I couldn't see any blood or obvious injuries so I decided to leave her. I ran over to the biker. It was weird, I remember it so vividly. He was laid straight with one arm casually draped over his chest and the other by his side. He could have been taking a nap in the morning sun. I bent over him, trying desperately to remember any emergency first aid – don't move him, don't take the helmet off – but the minute I lifted his visor I realised that all the first aid in the world was irrelevant at that point. His skin was grey and his eyes were shut but the most shocking thing was the noise. He was breathing hard and every breath sounded like a grunt, like he was taking a hard punch to the stomach. I knew it was pointless to ask him if he was okay; he was in some dark place losing the fight of his life. This being the days before universal mobile phones, I flagged some cars down, and sent a man to find a phone and get an ambulance. By now a crowd was starting to gather and someone shouted 'Let me through, I'm a doctor'. I drifted to the edge of the group and waited around for a while. I remember speaking to a policeman, giving my name and address, getting back in my car, driving to work, sitting at my desk and bursting into tears. I couldn't leave because I was shaking too much to drive the 20 mile journey home and in any case I couldn't face the thought until I had regained my composure of collecting my tiny daughter from the childminders. With all my appointments quickly rearranged by concerned colleagues, my boss took me under his wing and made me accompany him on all his visits instead, though it is all a bit of a blur now. In the paper it said a lorry had switched lanes without signaling causing the woman to swerve. She hit the bike and the bike hit the kerb. The rider was catapulted head first into a lamp post. He died later that morning from head injuries. I never was much interested in motorbikes after that. This, in a way, was a pity because when I was growing up my dad always had first scooters and then motorbikes. In fact, when I was two years old my dad used to take me to nursery on the back of his scooter. 'Your nana knit you some lovely thick socks that went over your shoes and some big mittens like baby gauntlets, to keep your hands warm' says my mum. Then, as the family got bigger he moved on to a motorbike and sidecar. We didn't get our first family car until I was a teenager. Even then I remember thinking that driving around in our pea green Ford Prefect was never going to be as much fun as standing on the seat in the sidecar with the roof rolled back as we raced across the Yorkshire Moors. I can still remember the sheer breathtaking feel of wind in my face and the effort needed not to laugh out loud or scream with joy because having your mouth open meant flies for dinner. My dad was not a fanatic though and saw motorbikes merely as a means of transport, that could easily be replaced when cars became more affordable. One of my early boyfriends had a small machine, I don't remember what make it was, but it was dirty and noisy. He took me out once on pillion and my only real memory of that occasion was when he dropped me off and said 'I'm not doing that again, you're hopeless at leaning – you have to lean with me.' It might have helped if he had explained that before we set off and then when the bike leaned to one side I wouldn't have been leaning to the other, trying to be helpful and act as a counterbalance in case we toppled over! How are people supposed to know about these things? So, mixed memories, all put into long-term storage on the day I witnessed the motorbike accident.

Then, a couple of years ago my husband came back from a conference where he had been talking to an old colleague of ours who is now in her 70's. She said to him that the worst thing about getting old is that your mind still wants to do things but your body doesn't. She told him he should get on and do the things he

wanted to do before he was too old! 'Like what?' I said.
'Well, like all those things I've always wanted to do but not quite
got around to.' 'Which are?' Conversations are often done in this
step by step, pulling teeth sort of a way with my husband. Still, I
persevered. 'Which are?' With a wistful look in his eye, he said
'Well for one thing, I've always wanted to ride a motorbike.'
'A motorbike?' Fortunately that is a word you can still say clearly
when your jaw has dropped. Then we had that conversation that
everyone has at one time or another which goes something like
... ' But that's dangerous, you could be killed' followed by 'Look
crossing the road is dangerous, I could be run over by a bus
tomorrow' and so on. It's the argument that everything in life is a
potential death trap versus where is the joy in living a life that is
totally risk free? I could see he wasn't going to be put off by my
scaremongering about certain death so, being a woman and full of
guile, I decided to try another tack. 'But Mike, you're still young,
you've got plenty of time to do all the things you want to do, why
rush into this now, why not start with something a bit easier?' He
faltered momentarily, caught off guard by the phrase 'you're still
young'. Then wearing the smile that he saves for small children
and innocents, he said '49 might seem young to you but I'm 50
next year and that's old'. The funny thing was, when he said that
he did look old, just for a second. So I switched to tack number
three. 'Well how are you going to learn to ride a motorbike? What
do you have to do and, more importantly, can you afford to do it?'
This is where we women sometimes get it wrong with our men
folk because we fail to spot the frontier between 'it was only an
idea' territory and 'I am definitely going to do this' territory and
then accidentally push them over it. We mistakenly think that if
we point out all the problems and pitfalls our husbands will come
to their senses and drop whatever mad scheme they are dreaming

up next. But it doesn't work like that and, too late I realised that all my questions and objections were actually strengthening his resolve and not weakening it. When he looked at me, grinned and said 'I don't know but I'm going to find out' I knew it was a lost cause. I have to admit though looking at him standing there, mulling over this idea, he did look younger but that was probably due to the effects of a small testosterone surge that I suspect he was experiencing at that moment. 'Fine, it's your life but don't expect me to join in' I said, wondering if this last, almost throwaway remark might put him off. You see, we do nearly everything together. We work together and we play together, we are not used to doing things on our own. This is not some sickly, 'joined at the hip' kind of relationship, it's just that we're best mates and prefer each other's company, most of the time, to anyone else's so this was going to be interesting.

The husband cracks it

Success seems to be largely a matter of hanging on after others have let go.
William Feather

Having now decided that he wanted to learn to ride a motorbike, Mike spent the next few nights researching how to do this on the internet. I was not impressed, however, as mid life crises go I suppose this was better than chasing after other women or spending endless days on the golf course. It is very hard, though, when you love someone, and you have powerful memories of seeing someone else killed in a motorbike accident, to be enthusiastic and supportive about them choosing to do things that seem so obviously dangerous, even life threatening. However, he was determined and nothing I could say or do was going to change his mind and a couple of weeks later he went off to do his Compulsory Basic Training at the local bike school. Not having the right gear, he decided to wear an old waterproof anorak, some jeans and his thick soled shoes. It was a warm day so he looked a bit ridiculous but when I pointed this out he gave me a withering look and said 'Look, it's going to be cold on the bikes and I need as much protection as I can get if I fall off.' It struck me then that he had been giving this whole venture some real thought so I shut up, gave him a kiss and said those reassuring words 'Try not to kill yourself' just to make him feel a little bit guilty about ignoring my pleas to drop the whole idea. So off he went. I got on with all those interesting Saturday activities like shopping, doing the washing and pottering around the garden but all the time wondering how he was getting on and hoping, I hate to admit this, that he was finding it really difficult and no fun and was wondering why he had put himself through this ordeal in the first place. No such luck.

Around teatime he strolled into the house looking tired and a bit wind blown but with an air of achievement about him. 'How did it go?' I asked. 'Well it was very good actually; they cover everything with you, and put loads of effort into showing you how to keep yourself safe on the road.' I couldn't resist – 'Well that's not surprising is it when you think how dangerous it is, I mean people get killed on motorbikes all the time.' He just ignored this and, as he stood washing his hands at the kitchen sink, he went on to explain 'Well, no that's not true actually, it's got a lot safer since this training was introduced and there have been fewer deaths. Besides which only older guys like me can afford to insure bikes these days so there are not so many young hotheads around.' Suddenly, in my mind's eye, I had an image of loads of middle-aged men, potbellies squeezed into tight leathers posing as young bucks on their Harley Davidsons, semi naked women hanging around their necks. I hate that, the semi naked women bit that is, because who in their right mind is going to jump on the back of someone's motorbike and tear off into the sunset wearing only a leather thong? Well obviously some people do, the image has to come from somewhere, but, I mean, it's ridiculous isn't it? Anyway, that aside I now wanted to know whether this urge to ride a motorbike had burnt itself out in the oxygen of experience. Well, had it? No. Not only had he gone ahead and booked a Direct Access Course to learn how to ride a bigger bike but he had also got an application form for his theory test. 'My God', I thought, 'he's really going to do this.' I carefully composed my 'disappointed in you' look – the one I usually keep for the kids when they do something that really upset me. 'So, you're going to carry on then?' He missed or chose to ignore my disapproving tone and said 'Yes, yes I am. It's a challenge and I'm enjoying learning something new and want to see if I can do this.' I had to admit to myself that I was not going to win this one so I withdrew. 'Fine. Good luck with it then.' This he heard thanks to that filtering mechanism adopted by most men, selective deafness, and turning to face me he grinned and said 'Don't worry, I'm going to take care, I'm not going to kill myself' and he gave me a big hug, a peck on the cheek and said 'Now, what's for tea?'

Over the next few weeks he took his Direct Access Course. I can't remember how many lessons over how many days but he persevered. Some days he came home buzzing with it all and other days he looked completely exhausted and dispirited. How he was doing this, with no practice in between lessons, as he didn't have a motorbike, I don't know. For a couple of evenings he worked through the riding theory questions on the computer and then drove off to the local test centre to sit the theory test. He rang me from his mobile phone. 'I passed' he said matter of factly like it was never in doubt. 'Well done' I said cheerfully, thinking 'Oh my god, another step closer to an early grave.'

On the day of his road test he was more nervous than I had seen him in a while, in fact, since the day he had rung up to resign from a well paid job that was making him ill. He kept checking that he had got the correct paperwork with him, and looking out of the window at the sky. It was a cloudy day with rain threatening but, according to the weather forecast, it promised to clear up later. Finally he left to drive to the bike school to meet with his instructor, to collect his bike and ride to the test centre, 20 miles away. I waited by the phone. What time was his test again? 10.30 or was it 10.45? No one rang. 'He's failed' I thought 'Well either that or he's been killed on the road, or he would have rung me'. Whilst I was mulling this over the door opened and in he walked looking fed up. 'What happened - did you pass?' I asked. 'No it was postponed because it was too windy to ride'. Too windy to ride? It had never entered my head that that sort of thing could happen. So all that anxiety and nervousness was for nothing. Then, for just a moment, I felt real admiration for his doggedness with this whole business. He was determined to see this through and see it through he did. The following week he took his test and failed, comforting himself with his instructors comments that hardly anyone passes first time. A couple of weeks after that, with a new test date, he woke up with a head cold, dragged himself off to the bike school, skipped his lesson and went straight to the test and passed. I was so proud of him, though of course still disapproved strongly of what he was doing. But to pass like that in such a short time, with hardly any practice, well that's why I married him because he's smart and determined and he growls in the face of adversity … okay so maybe I did get a bit over excited. However, I quickly came down to earth when he said 'And now I've got to go and sort out a helmet and gloves.' 'Why?' I said, already knowing deep down what was coming next. 'Why? Because I've just bought a motorbike. It belongs to one of the instructors, it's a Honda CB500, just like the one I trained on and I can now start to really learn how to ride!' I knew it. This was a bad dream that I was not going to wake up from.

Lock up your bikes!

It's not a big motorcycle, just a groovy little motorbike.
Little Honda, The Beach Boys

The following weekend I was just tidying up the kitchen after breakfast when the doorbell rang. I opened the door and standing there was a tall, smiling Adonis of a man covered in leather from head to toe. 'Hi, I'm Mark, is Mike around?' he said. 'Yes, come in, I'll go get him.' I showed him into the living room and then went to the bottom of the stairs. I was tempted for a second to call out 'Mike your friend's here – he wants to know if you're coming out to play' but then thought better of it. 'MIKE, MARK'S HERE WITH THE BIKE' I yelled. I went back into the living room where Mark was standing looking out through the French windows. It suddenly struck me that he might be uncomfortable about sitting down in his biking leathers so I said 'It's okay to sit down you know, do you want a cup of tea or coffee? He smiled politely, 'Coffee would be nice, thanks'. What a nice man, so polite and friendly. As I went off to make the coffee I had to remind myself that this was the enemy, the man who was bringing the machine that might kill my loved one but it's hard to scowl at an open, smiling face. When I got back to the living room, Mike and Mark were talking about the bike, when it was last serviced, how it performed and so on. I plonked down the drinks and was about to leave when I noticed how excited Mike was. He's not the most expressive of people but when he's happy or excited he gets a sort of look on his face and he talks in a more animated way. He was loving this. Mark, on the other hand, looked a bit tired and fed up and we soon found out why. Apparently he owned about six different motorbikes which he kept in his garage. The night before someone had broken in and tried to steal one of them. Mark explained: 'Fortunately, it was chained to the floor: I had a big metal ring concreted into the garage floor about three months ago and the bike was chained to that so they couldn't get it. They tried to smash the ring and left some nice gouges in the concrete and the bike got knocked about a bit but they finally gave up and left.' I was shocked. 'Were all the bikes chained down?' I asked. 'No, only the Aprillia. They weren't interested in the others. My guess is, it was a steal to order job and they only wanted the Aprillia.' Looking over at me and seeing my shocked expression, Mark then tried to reassure me by saying 'This sort of thing happens all the time. One guy I know parked his Aprillia right at the back of his garage with his car in front of it and even that got nicked. The police think the only way they could have done it was to have a team of them on the job. They broke into the garage and then lifted the bike up and over the top of the car before making off with it.' I was not reassured. Also I didn't know what an Aprillia was but, guessing that it must be an expensive motorbike, I acted like I did. This glimpse into the murky underworld of biking left me a bit stunned. I never knew people were that interested in bikes; I thought they were just speed machines that blokes liked to whizz around on. Stealing to order?

Once the buying and selling business was over and Mark had given Mike a guided tour of the bike, Mike gave Mark a lift home in the car. I was left alone with the bike. Having tried to act disinterested so far, I now decided to sneak a good look at it whilst Mike's back was turned. The bike looked big and menacing to me. The paintwork was a greeny grey colour with flashes of yellow, the petrol tank bulged up like the muscle bound back of a powerful animal, crouched ready to launch itself into the chase and the back end seemed to taper away to nothing. It was not the most beautiful of bikes and standing there on our drive it exuded power. I shuddered and went inside. When Mike got back he spent a few minutes looking the bike over and then came in to make a cup of tea. I quickly sussed out that he had decided to play this whole thing very low key with me. Sort of 'don't act excited, don't go on about the bike 'cos the missus will only get upset.' I decided to go along with this and said nothing. He cracked first. 'Have you had a look at the bike then?' he said as he boiled the kettle. 'Yes' I said in as disinterested a tone as I could muster. 'What do you think?' He was obviously trying to gently acclimatise me to this new addition to our family. I noticed he was using the same approach to me that my eldest daughter Kathryn used when she brought home a kitten which 'reeeeaaaally needed a home, please mum? ' Am I that easy to sucker? I wondered. 'What do I think? … I'm not sure what I think and, in any case, what does it matter what I think, it's your bike' I said. At that moment I looked at him and saw that he really did want my approval, after all I'm his best mate and mates should stick together. With a sigh, I said 'Okay let's go and have a look at it' and out we trundled to do the guided tour of the bike, together. Later that morning he put on his new helmet and gloves and took the bike out. As I watched him wobble off the drive I realised that he really was a novice rider and would have to do a lot of riding to gain that easy, 'throw your leg over the machine and zoom off' style that the bikers I saw in the petrol station seemed to have. Over the next few weeks each time he went out I kept myself busy but watched the clock, thinking things like 'How long has he been gone now? Where did he say he was going?' I was on edge the whole time he was out. Then every time he wobbled back onto the drive I felt a surge of relief wash over me, my gratitude that he had, once again, avoided death's clutches making me almost ache with love for him. This was soon forgotten though when he wrestled the bike round to the back of the house and parked it on the patio right outside the French windows. 'You're not leaving it there are you?' quickly turned into 'YOU ARE NOT LEAVING IT THERE!' It was ridiculous. After a hard days work you want to settle down on the settee with a nice cup of tea and look out over.. what? Well over the patio and garden obviously, not the forecourt of a motorbike showroom. 'It's just for now till I decide where to keep it' he said. One thing I've learnt about men, well this man, is that 'just for now' can quickly turn into 'just for ever' if I let it so after a short but intense nagging campaign on my behalf he bought a bike cover and moved it to the path round the side of the house. This didn't seem very safe to me, especially in light of Mark's stories, but what could we do? We didn't have a garage and it was not staying on the patio!

Then Mike stopped going out on the bike as the weather got worse in late autumn and winter and it was stashed away under its bright green cover. We got on with our lives and, for a while, this whole motorbiking business was dropped. If it hadn't been for the big green lump standing on the back path, which we had to squeeze round every time we went up the garden for logs for the fire, I think we would have forgotten all about the bike. Then it was suddenly spring again and spring always brings me out into the garden. I love gardening and spend as much time as I can pottering about in ours. Of course, that year I had to keep squeezing past the big green lump, with my garden trug full of weeds, to get to the compost bin by the back hedge. 'When are you going to go out on that bike again, now the weathers okay?' I asked him. Every time I asked him this he came back with one excuse or another. 'The weather's still a bit chilly' or 'I'm too busy today' or 'It's been standing outside all winter so I really need to get it serviced first' and so on. Now I'm from Yorkshire and was brought up to abhor waste of any kind. That machine had cost a lot of money and there it was merrily rusting away in the back garden. In spite of my objections to biking I couldn't bear to see money wasted in this way. I confronted him. 'Look, if you're not going to ride it you ought to sell it. Why don't you go out on it?' Looking back I cannot believe I was encouraging him to go out biking but I was and then the truth came out. 'Oh stop going on about it, I'm not even sure I want to go out on it that much. I'm fed up of just riding around in circles, on my own. If I had someone to go with and somewhere I really wanted to get to then that might be different ..' I could hear the frustration in his voice. So that was the real reason he was not going out much. 'Well why don't you join a bikers club?' Even as I said this I knew this wasn't the answer. Quick as a flash he came back at me, 'I don't want to, they're full of speed nuts and real fanatics and I'm not either of those. Maybe I should sell it.' This last bit was said in a sad, resigned way. I think he genuinely did want to keep biking but not on his own. Then I said something that to this day I cannot believe I said; 'Maybe I should have a go and see if I can do it and then we could go out together.' What was I thinking? He laughed out loud. 'You are joking aren't you? You hate bikes.' He was right, I did hate bikes but I loved him and we did do most things together and maybe I owed it to him to have a try. I still can't believe I said that. Anyway, one thing led to another and a couple of weeks later I was signed up for my Compulsory Basic Training at the local bike school.

And before you even sit on a bike...

To become a better rider, we have to recognize the resistance in ourselves to accepting responsibility, and take steps to overcome it. The first step is to recognize that we all have a resistance to learning.
Motorcycle Roadcraft: The Police Rider's Handbook

So there I was all kitted out in my old waterproof anorak, jeans and thick soled shoes and looking just as ridiculous as Mike had on his basic training day. More so, in fact, because I had lost a lot of weight the previous year so my bright red anorak hung off me like a sack. He, however, didn't make any comment knowing that it wouldn't take much for me to pick up the phone and cancel. I was very nervous but kept reminding myself of what mum used to say when she gave us a new vegetable for tea. My sister and brother and I would look at the broccoli on our plate and then at her before moaning 'Do we have to?' and her response was always the same. 'How will you know you don't like it if you don't try it?' Mike was busy making me a packed lunch and I was spending my time either wandering around wringing my hands or going to the loo. Mike called from the kitchen 'Look, you'll be fine, they take good care of you, you'll be with an instructor all the time. In any case you learn how to handle the bike in the car park before you go out on the road'. I wandered in to stand next to him and calm down. He is very good at keeping steady under pressure. We run a small business together and in the months when sales are poor he's the one who says things like 'It's okay, things will pick up, just relax' whilst I run around wailing and tearing out my hair. He then went on to tell me about his basic training day. 'There was a woman in the group and she really struggled to handle the bike. She kept losing her balance and falling off in the car park. Eventually, after a discussion with the instructor she withdrew from the course at lunch time before we went out on the road.' I listened to this and felt relieved, knowing I could stop at any point if I felt out of my depth. 'So if I want to pack it in I can' I said but even as I said it I felt the stirrings of determination in the pit of my stomach. 'You won't have any problems like that, you ride bicycles all the time, you've got great balance on two wheels' Mike stated matter of factly as he buttered the bread. I loved him at times like that. He might not be much of a talker and sometimes he talks absolute rubbish but every once in a while he says just the right thing. 'That's right, I do ride bicycles, I will be fine, I mean these motorbikes are just like motorised bicycles aren't they?' Mike gave me a doubtful look at that point but said nothing.

So off we went. Mike took me up to the school; we parked up and went in together. He started chatting with the instructors, Danny and Ian, and then introduced me. I felt so tiny standing there, all five foot six inches of me, alongside these big blokes all wearing biking gear. Danny focused his attention on me, 'Are you okay?' I think I must have looked terrified but I said 'I'm fine', as you do. Then he just kept looking at me and smiling so I felt compelled to admit that I was a bit nervous, well very nervous, well actually, terrified but I did ride bicycles. Danny looked at me the way you look at children and non-English speakers when they have said something incomprehensible and then said 'Well, yes, I'm sure you'll be fine.' At this point Mike piped up and said 'Maybe it would be better if she just trained on an automatic.' It took me a minute to work out what he was saying. He was suggesting I learn to ride a scooter, which I imagine would be easier. I suddenly felt indignant. What was he saying, that I wasn't good enough to ride a motorbike with gears? Something inside me snapped. I turned to him and, in unison with Danny, said 'No'. I turned and looked at Danny. Once again he was looking at me and smiling. 'No' he said, 'I think she should have a go on the bikes with the gears and see how she gets on, we don't want to limit her options at this stage'. I turned back to smirk at Mike and thought 'This guy Danny is okay.' Eventually everyone in that day's CBT group arrived, the three other blokes doing the training and Lee, our tall, blond instructor for the day. He introduced himself and got us to introduce ourselves and then we got started. The morning was spent in a room full of mismatched and battered armchairs going through the health and safety procedures. We began by watching a video called 'I'm sorry I didn't see you' in which a motorcyclist gets knocked off his bike. Good start eh? This was followed by a talk on what to wear. I began to realise how important the clothing was as we talked about fabrics and how leather breathes but isn't waterproof; man made fibres are waterproof but might make you feel a bit sweaty; black might be sexy but it doesn't make you easy to see and so on. We even talked about things like zips needing to have flaps over them otherwise wind and rain can seep through. We looked at the inside section of a crash helmet, as Lee had one that had been cut in half, and talked about what happens to the polystyrene lining if you drop the helmet and why you need to replace it. We looked at how to keep your visor clean and how important it was to choose the right size helmet. Then we went on to footwear. 'Don't wear shoes or boots with laces if you can help it' said Lee 'in case they get loose and get wrapped round something.' He also explained that it was a good idea to wear boots because the stone that can shatter your windscreen might just shatter your shinbone. Once we had covered all the clothing we talked about basic maintenance of a bike and all the things you need to check regularly to keep your bike in good working order. We also talked about different road surfaces and how to take extra care when riding over things like the white lines and manhole covers because they can be very slippery when they are wet. Then we were told to watch another video and see if we could spot the hazards on the road as the camera moved along it. It soon became apparent that nearly everything was a hazard! Lee then told us something which has stuck with me ever since. 'When you're riding a motorbike you have to assume that everyone else on the road is trying to kill you. You have to ride defensively at all times'. Sobering stuff but actually I felt reassured because I found it easy to respond naturally to all this talk about keeping ourselves safe. If they had been talking about the joy of speed, the fun of zooming round corners and scraping your knee on the tarmac I would probably have freaked out. When we broke for lunch I was feeling more relaxed but as I sat eating my sandwiches and drinking my tea I could hear Danny and Lee discussing who was going to be put on which bikes in the afternoon and my stomach began to tighten.

Motorbike riding as comic spectacle

You have to stop worrying about looking foolish, 'cause fear of being humiliated really limits you.
Dean Koontz, Fear Nothing

After lunch we had to choose a helmet from a collection on a rack by the door and I had to try on a few to find one that was the right size. Taking them on and off was a nuisance and I quickly learnt that helmets and earrings don't go well together. Eventually I found a helmet that fit me and put it on. It was hot and stuffy inside and I could almost smell the sweat from all those earlier nervous wearers. Next I picked out some gloves. The only ones that fit me smelt horrible and felt sticky but I decided not to comment as no one else seemed bothered by things like this. Then we went out to the car park. The bike school is located at the bottom end of an industrial estate and most of the units seemed to be closed or closing by the time we came out. This meant that we had the use of quite a large car park. Lined up in a row were four motorbikes – two little ones and two quite big ones like the one Mike had bought. I dashed over and laid claim to the smallest one – a nice little Yamaha 125cc with a low seat and an upright seating position. One of the other learners, called John, had told me over lunch that he only wanted to learn to ride because he and his wife had just had a baby and she now needed the car so that she could drop their child off at nursery on her way to work. John's idea was to do the basic training and get a little bike that would take him the seven miles to work and back. He chose the other 125cc next to mine. The other blokes, Darren and Mark, sauntered over to the big bikes. Darren had done a lot of off road speedway riding so was very familiar with bikes but still had to do this course and the Direct Access course to be eligible to ride on the road. He instantly looked comfortable in the saddle. Mark, well Mark struck me as a speed nut in the making. He tried to look like he too was very confident with bikes but then throughout the afternoon kept making silly mistakes and going a bit too fast. I think testosterone was affecting his judgment. We began by just sitting on the bikes and getting familiar with the controls. I had to keep telling myself to relax. We had to get on and off the bikes, push them around and then put them on their side stands and take them off again. Mine felt heavy but manageable. Then we had to get on and start them up. It was quite hard to listen to Lee's instructions and look down at the bike controls with the helmet on and I really had to concentrate. Once Lee was happy that we knew how to stop and start the bike and work the gears we were told to just ride in a circle around the car park. I set off, erratically lurching and stopping, lurching and stopping, kangarooing my way along. It was really hard trying to set off smoothly and my little bike felt incredibly powerful to me as I let out the clutch and surged forward. I say surged but on reflection I could have walked quicker round that car park. Lee was calling to me 'C'mon Jackie, get some speed up' but I resolutely stuck to my first gear and churned my way around the car park. The traffic cones loomed ahead of me, I knew I had to go round them but accelerating and steering so soon, surely that was too much to expect of anyone? Actually, it wasn't, because the other guys were merrily riding around the cones and lapping me at regular intervals, but I tried not to look at them because that just made me feel even more hopeless. Eventually I managed to go round slowly but steadily and once even got into second gear. Mind you that was only after I was reminded that the gear pedal has to be flicked up to go up the gears. I had been banging it down every time I got up a bit of speed and of course that just put me back into first gear again. For a while I thought I had gone up to second gear and was thinking how little difference there was between first and second gear when Lee noticed what I was doing and he shouted 'Flick the pedal up Jackie for second gear'. Why did he have to shout it out like that in front of the others? I grinned sheepishly at them, which of course they didn't see because of the helmet, but as I tootled past Darren, finally in second gear, he said to me 'You're doing great Jackie' and I was really chuffed. I knew it was just kind words to the lost and hopeless but hell, every little helps.

Then things got a lot harder. We had to ride figures of eight round the traffic cones. 'Look where you want the bike to go and the bike will go round' explained Lee. It was a lot harder than it sounded because the idea of not looking straight ahead was very, very scary. It reminded me of when I was a kid learning to ride a bicycle and my dad, running beside me with his hand holding the back of my saddle, saying 'Stop looking at the pedals Jackie and watch where you're going!' For some reason I just couldn't drag my eyes off the pedals, I don't know why and it was the same with the motorbike. For some reason I just couldn't pull my head around from the 'eyes fixed to the front' position. This meant that I ended up doing figures of nine, figures of six and figures of zero with the very occasional lopsided figure of eight. By this time, the other lads were riding smoothly round the obstacle course in about half a minute and then they would line up their bikes and watch my ragged attempts which took anything up to about two minutes. It was so embarrassing. I said to Lee 'Can't they get on with something else whilst I practice this?' thinking that by the time I'd mastered these manoeuvres they could have prepared a one hour trick cycling demonstration. I felt like someone in a microlight trying to take part in a Red Arrows display. 'Don't worry about them, concentrate on what you're doing, you're doing fine' said Lee, smiling. Then things got worse. I kept stalling the bike and at one point it took me about twenty five goes to get it started again. Lee stood over me saying 'Okay, put it into first, ease out the clutch and now give it some revs Jackie'. I was doing this, I was, but it kept stalling. 'Lee, go away, just leave me alone, I need to do this on my own. Go and teach them to do something else' I said, hoping he would go off and distract my increasingly bored and restless audience. At this point I had an angry conversation with myself which went something like 'Look, concentrate you idiot. You can do this, you've been doing it already. Just get this bike started and drive it round the bloody car park!' Getting angry with myself in this way actually helped and I managed to get the bike going and do the rest of the manoeuvers. These included pulling up to pretend junctions, marked out with the traffic cones, and turning right, stopping and setting off and so on, in preparation for going out on the road after a short tea break.

Over tea I felt exhausted and a bit disheartened but Darren came and sat by me and asked me why I wanted to learn to ride. I told him about Mike and the bike and then he said 'I really admire what you're doing. My wife would never do anything like that and I think you could get good at this. Wait till you go out on the road, you'll probably surprise yourself, I think with a bit more riding and a bit more confidence you're going to be okay at this.' I looked at him with his shaved head and his tattooed arms and thought 'This guy is really nice.' How strange, I would never normally speak to someone like this, not because I would go out of my way to avoid them but because our paths would never cross. 'Thanks Darren' I said with a sigh, 'it's nice to know somebody thinks I can do it because I'm certainly not sure.'

Then we each got kitted out with a radio mic to link us to the instructors. By this time another man had turned up on a Honda Goldwing, which is a motorbike that looks like a huge armchair on two wheels. He took Darren and Mark out, John and I went with Lee. They had obviously worked out which was the fast group and which was the remedial group. Off we went; first into the industrial estate to practice emergency stops which I managed to do okay being an expert at stopping already; U-turns which I managed after a fashion and road positioning for turning which I also managed after a fashion. Then out onto the road. John went in front, then me, then Lee bringing up the rear. Lee wore a fluorescent waistcoat over his bike gear with the word INSTRUCTOR clearly printed on the back. We had RIDER UNDER INSTRUCTION on our jackets though mine might more appropriately have said WARNING - COMPLETE CLUTZ. We rode round the town and up and down housing estates where Lee had to constantly remind me to switch off my indicator, though why they don't go off automatically like they do in a car I don't know. Then we rode along the ring road where Lee's voice told us we had to get up some speed. It was this last bit that was the most fun. Just going straight along a dual carriageway, where people could overtake you was relatively easy to do and for the first time I felt a bit thrilled. I wanted to laugh out loud but worried that Lee might hear me on the headphones, I wasn't sure if they were two way or not, so I kept it in but I had to admit I was enjoying this, just a bit.

After managing to do a hill start and get round a roundabout, with lots of traffic lights, in busy traffic we made our way back to the bike school. I parked up and pulled off the sweaty helmet and couldn't stop grinning. I had done it. By this time Mike had turned up to take me home. 'How did she get on?' he asked Lee, obviously not trusting me to give a balanced appraisal of my own performance. 'She was okay. I am going to pass her but she does lack confidence and she needs to remember to switch off her indicator. I think, though, that with practice she could get good at this, what do you think Jackie?' He turned to me. 'Yes, it was fun' I said in a tired voice, thinking to myself 'It was fun, wasn't it?' To be honest I was exhausted and wasn't sure what to think. Then Danny piped up, 'So, are you going to do the Direct Access Course then, get yourself onto a bigger motorbike and do your test?' I had decided I liked Danny but when he said that I thought 'This guy is insane.' A Direct Access Course, a bigger bike, was he mad? 'Er no, I don't think so, those 125cc are pretty powerful and I wouldn't want to go on anything bigger than that.' The blokes all looked amused and I think Mike even sniggered but I was too tired to argue. So I got my certificate, said my thankyous and goodbyes and collapsed in the car dreaming of a hot bath and a glass of wine.

A cool cruiser for a cool hen

I knew, my core knew that I would never be the same again, could never be the same again. A motorcycle. All that from a collection of bolts and nuts and metal and paint but more, more than that. Gary Paulsen, Zero to Sixty: A Motorcycle Journey of a Lifetime

Lying in the bath, I mulled over the day and realised that I had actually enjoyed it. Not in an 'Oh, isn't this fun, aren't we having a lovely time' sort of way but more in a 'This is scary and thrilling and a real challenge' sort of a way. I imagine it's a bit like how people feel when they do the white knuckle rides at places like Alton Towers. As they step down from the ride they say 'That was great' whilst looking relieved that it's over but chuffed with themselves for having done it. I never ride those things so I wouldn't know but I would guess it's a pretty similar feeling. I felt really proud of myself even though I had been the out and out dunce in the class. So what to do now? I certainly wasn't going to try and ride a bigger bike as the little ones still scared me rigid, so the Direct Access Course was out. No, what I needed was to get more practice on a 125cc. How would I do that? Could you hire them for long periods or rent them out on a daily basis? I wondered.

'Mike, can you hire or rent out small motorbikes?' I asked him later that evening as we relaxed in front of the TV. 'I don't know, why?' He looked at me with a quizzical expression on his face. 'Well I was thinking I might like to try and get a bit more practice in' I said. He thought for a moment. 'I don't know, I've never heard of anyone doing that.' As he said this I noticed that he was looking at me with a strange expression on his face. 'What?' I said. He then said a phrase, which over the next few weeks became almost a catch phrase for him. 'You've changed your tune.' That's the catchphrase. 'I thought you hated bikes and now you want to hire one and get some practice in.' He laughed and shook his head as if to say 'What am I going to do with her?' I ignored this as my mind was now beginning to wrestle with the problem of how to practice riding a motorbike when I didn't have one to ride. I was going to have to buy one. 'Mike, how do you buy a motorbike?' He carried on shaking his head in mock disbelief but with a little smile playing on his lips he said 'What do you mean, how do you buy a motorbike? You buy a motorbike like you'd buy anything else – from someone that wants to sell one.' I could see that this was going to be another one of those teeth pulling conversations. 'I know that, but where can you buy one round here?' Before we could get much further with this step by step guide to buying motorbikes in our area, Mike looked at me hard and said 'You're going to buy a motorbike?' I nodded. 'You've changed your tune.' I came to hate that phrase, I really came to hate that phrase. 'It's a woman's prerogative to change her mind' I said, hoping that would be the end of it. Chuckling, he said 'You've really changed your tune.' I could feel my eyes beginning to roll up into the top of my head with exasperation and knew that I would have to give him a bit more time to get used to this new idea of me buying a motorbike. He's never been very good at quick changes, he doesn't trust them. Getting Mike to change direction on almost anything is a bit like trying to turn a tanker. 'It's a nice day, let's go for a walk' I might say. 'But I thought we were going shopping?' he replies, looking confused. 'I know, but it is such a lovely day, let's forget the shopping and go for a walk' I say. 'But what about the shopping, I thought we'd agreed we were doing that?' he says, and so it goes on. He likes to be certain and know what is coming next so this whole thing with me and the motorbike was rocking his boat quite a bit. I decided to leave it alone for a while and let him mull it over and get used to the idea.

Sure enough, a couple of days later he brought in a copy of Bike Trader magazine, handed it over to me and said 'You might find something in there that would be okay'. 'Good man, he's coming round' I thought feeling excited, because when Mike and I pool our energies on a project we are famous in our family for getting things done. My mum often says things like 'I don't know, you're always up to something you two, I don't know how you manage to do it all.' So if he was going to help me with this, it was definitely going to happen. I flicked through the pages getting more and more excited. All these machines for sale, so many to choose from, but then I remembered I needed to focus on the 125cc's. This narrowed down the choice somewhat and as I looked carefully at the small bikes I realised that I couldn't do it this way. I needed to see the bikes and sit on them and get a feel for them. All these different names and makes - Hondas, Kawasakis, Ducatis - didn't mean a thing to me. The only bikes that I had any feeling for were Yamahas, because I had trained on one, and Harley Davidsons because, well everyone has heard of Harley Davidsons. As I looked at the Harleys with their wonderful names like Fat Boy and Softail, I remembered seeing a girl on one once. I was queuing at the traffic lights at the end of our road and she pulled up alongside me. She was all in leather but her long blond hair spilled out down her back from under her helmet which was the same colour as the petrol tank on her sparkling blue and chrome Harley. She looked fantastic. I remembered thinking 'A cool chick on a cool cruiser'. Nice. Then I suddenly had a thought 'That could be me.' Well maybe not, as I was probably old enough to be her mother. Well, never mind, perhaps I could be a cool hen on a cool cruiser. I had never been a cool anything in my life before, I was too noisy and excitable, but this could be my chance. Yes, I decided, I needed to get a cruiser. I told Mike. 'A cruiser; a 125cc cruiser? What do you want a cruiser for?' he asked. I decided not to mention the cool hen thing so instead, thinking rapidly, I said 'Well, I think I would feel safer on a cruiser because I could get both my feet on the ground.' He looked at me suspiciously. 'Both your feet on the ground?' I decided it wasn't wise to persist with this in case he winkled the cool hen thing out of me so I switched tack. 'Look, never mind that, where can we go and see some bikes and try them out because I need to do that before I can make any decisions.' He thought for a moment and then said that there was a place about twenty miles away that had a big selection so we could go up there and have a look round. So the next weekend that's what we did.

The search is over

Women riding motorcycles isn't really an issue per se anymore. What is important are the specific concerns that many of the women talk about ... a lot of the women feel isolated ... some women feel intimidated walking into bike shops ... what kind of bike is the best bike to start out with?'
Sister Teresa's story from Ralph 'Sonny' Barger , Ridin' High
– Livin' Free, Hell-Raising Motorcycle Tales by Keith and Kent Zimmerman.

The bike showroom was on the lower ground floor at the back of a sort of warehouse building. The upstairs floor was devoted to clothing, biking equipment and accessories. You had to know it was there to find it because there was only a small sign outside. However, it didn't really need to advertise itself because of all the bikes coming and going through the entrance, like bees to a hive, making it pretty obvious that this was a place that attracted bikers. We parked up. Mike had wanted us ride up on his bike, as I had now been and bought a crash helmet and gloves, but there was no way I was riding pillion with him whilst he was still such a novice. It was far too dangerous in my mind and, 'In any case' I thought, 'I'm sure there is a knack to getting on and off the pillion and I haven't got it and it would be just my luck to get my leg stuck and fall off in front of a load of other bikers'. So in the end we drove up. The place was swarming with bikers, leathers everywhere and machines dotted all around the place. There was a mobile burger bar parked up in the car park doing a roaring trade in hotdogs, burgers and chips. It felt like coming to worship at the temple of biking. We went downstairs to look at the bikes. I had never seen so many motorbikes packed together in one place before. All clean and shining and whispering 'buy me.. buy me.. get me out of here and onto the open road…'. The bikes were all on their side stands so leaned slightly to one side. It reminded me of the domino trick, hit one and they all fall over except in this case they had all frozen at a 70 degree angle. People were milling around, mainly men but some women too and a few kids running around excitedly yelling 'Dad, look at this one ..' All around me, machines kept beeping. Mike said he thought it was something to do with their alarm systems. I watched as people lovingly gazed at the machines of their dreams. Salesmen were being called over to discuss the finer points of particular bikes and I could overhear phrases like linked braking, fuel injection and torque settings being tossed around. I began to get nervous as it was clear that these people really understood bikes, how they were built, what every little bit of the engine did and how they performed on the road and off it. I, on the other hand, knew nothing. Even Mike knew a bit about the technical stuff. He stopped by a Suzuki Bandit and said 'I wonder what the BHP is on this one.' I looked at it carefully but I couldn't see the letters BHP on it anywhere. 'Where is it?' I asked him. 'Where's what?' he said, still focussing on the bike. 'The BHP' I said 'I can't see it anywhere'. He looked at me like I had just landed from the planet Venus, 'What do you mean you can't see it? Of course you can't see it, it's the brake horse power you twit'. I was about to tell him not to call me a twit when a salesman came over. His badge read Dave. 'Need any help?' he asked. Mike turned to him and said 'Have you got any 125cc's? Not for me of course, it's the missus, she's after a 125.' Dave slowly pivoted around and scanned the rows of bikes. 'There are a couple of small trial bikes over there and the Hondas are good little commuter bikes and there's a Yamaha down at the front – it depends on what you're after really.' Dave was in his forties, a nice friendly face and not much taller than me. He didn't look at all threatening so I opened up to him. 'Actually I know nothing about bikes but I've passed my CBT and want to have a go so I thought I'd use my hard earned savings to buy myself a little bike.' He smiled at me and said 'Good for you. I've just done the same thing for my missus. She passed her CBT so I've bought her a 125 to get some practice on before she does her Direct Access Course. Then when she passes her test I'll sell the 125 and, although we know we'll lose a few quid it should still work out cheaper than paying for her to have riding lessons to get the practice.' I was warming to him and wanted to tell him the cool hen thing but Mike jumped in and said 'Let's have a look at them all and see what we think.' Dave left us to it and said he would pop back over when we had decided which ones were of interest. We started with the sporty ones, which I instantly disliked. 'Those are for adolescent boys to ride up muddy hills' I said. Mike raised his eyebrows and moved on. The Hondas were okay but looked a bit staid, not something a cool hen would ride.

Then just as I was beginning to give up hope of seeing anything, there she was. A beautiful little Yamaha Virago 125cc cruiser, she had a burgundy petrol tank and mudguards and sparkling chrome everywhere else. She was lovely. Her buttoned down leather seat was nice and low and the handlebars swept up and round a bit to allow the perfect riding position. I was mesmerised. 'Ooh, this one is nice, can I sit on it?' I asked excitedly. Mike went and got Dave who pulled it out of line for me. I sat on it and my heart sang. 'Yes, this is it, this is the one' I said, grinning and bouncing up and down on the saddle. 'But you haven't tried any of the others yet' said Mike looking a bit exasperated. He likes to really look into things before he buys, consider the options, get the facts and then make a rational decision, whereas I just go with my gut instinct. This way of doing things drives him mad at times because sometimes I buy things as soon as I see them and other times I don't buy anything at all because nothing feels right.

But this little Virago cruiser felt exactly right. I wanted it, I had to have it. Dave talked technicals with Mike whilst I stroked the saddle and looked in the wing mirrors. 'It's a V twin' I heard Dave say and thought that the V must stand for Virago and so wondered what it was twinned with. Then I realised it had kilometres per hour on the speedometer and not miles per hour and thought maybe it had something to do with that. Maybe there was a bike somewhere round the back exactly like this one but that had miles per hour on it instead. I asked Dave about the speedometer and he explained that this bike was what was known as a parallel import. Apparently Yamaha didn't make Virago's for here anymore so they had to be imported from stocks held abroad. I decided not to quiz him about the twin thing as it didn't seem to fit with what he was saying, which was a good thing because I later found out that a V twin is a type of engine! Dave went on to explain that they would put stickers on the speedometer face to show the miles per hour equivalents. I was not deterred, she was just what I wanted and I was determined to buy her. So we talked money and terms and extras like data tagging and L plates and then agreed a collection date and time the following week. As we drove away I couldn't begin to imagine how I was going to sleep for the next few days.

Bringing baby home

I took the long way back home. A whole bunch of pothole roads with speed bumps so I could avoid the highway. We only lived seven or eight miles apart, and it should've taken twenty minutes with traffic, but it took me quite a few hours. I won't even say how long.
Flaming Iguanas: An All-Girl Road Novel Thing. Erika Lopez

At last the day to collect the bike arrived. I woke up to find glorious sunshine pouring in through the bedroom window. It was perfect biking weather, which was a relief because the previous evening I'd asked Mike to ride the cruiser home from the garage for me. 'What? You want me to ride it back? Why? It's your bike, you ride it.' He looked concerned but this was obviously not about me and my rising panic about getting back on a motorbike but more about him being seen on a 125cc. 'Please. I can't ride it back here, I've forgotten how to ride and it's twenty miles on main roads.' I hated myself but I was pleading. 'Oh, you'll be fine, it'll all come flooding back to you the minute you get it on the road' he said and carried on reading the newspaper. What was the matter with him? Couldn't he see how terrified I was, I needed his help with this. 'Please Mike' I said in a quiet voice. He looked at me and at last seemed to comprehend how hard this was for me and said, with a sigh, 'Oh okay but I think you're being silly, it's your bike and you should ride it'. I knew this was true and had been giving it a lot of thought. How was I going to learn how to ride my lovely new bike if I didn't go out and ride it? I had a vague idea about what I could do, but more of that later.

So off we went, Mike with his biking gear, because by now he had bought a proper biking jacket and me with my money and insurance paperwork. I had contacted the same insurers Mike had used and when I rang them I got a nice girl who took my details, her voice sounding bored until she heard the kind of bike I had bought. 'Oh a Virago, they're nice they are, they're little cruisers, aren't they.' I began to wax lyrical about my little dream machine and she said 'Oh you'll love it but make the most of it, you won't have it for long.' I felt a knot in my stomach. Why wouldn't I have it for long? Was it something to do with the insurance or was she suggesting I would write it off in a crash or something? 'What do you mean?' I asked hesitantly. 'Well, it's only a 125cc isn't it, which is fine to get started but trust me, you'll soon want a bigger one' she said, a hint of playful conspiracy in her voice. 'Do you think so?' I said lowering my voice too – why were we whispering? She then went on to tell me all about her experiences of biking. She commuted to work on hers and had started with a scooter but had felt left out when the blokes she worked with started going out for rides at weekends and she didn't feel able to tag along. So she bought a small bike and then realised she needed a bigger one and she now rode a Yamaha FSZ600, whatever that was. I listened intently, thinking how nice it was to hear a woman talking about biking. Up to now I had got the impression that this was very much a man's thing. They picked the bikes, loved them, rode them, maintained them and cleaned them. The women, on the other hand, either waved them off at the garden gate or, if they were particularly daring, donned their own leathers and helmets and hopped on the back, as pillion passengers. This is probably a total misrepresentation of women in biking but nevertheless it's the impression I'd gained from seeing all those men zooming around the place. As I put down the phone I wondered 'Would I want a bigger bike?' Maybe I would but I couldn't see it at the moment. The thought of collecting my little one was, as my kids would say, doing my head in.

When we arrived at the bike showroom it was a bit quieter than last time, it being a week day and not a Saturday. That was a relief because it meant Mike would be able to ride the bike out of a quiet car park without having to dodge and weave his way through the usual swarm of machines. We went in and made our way over to Dave the salesman. 'Morning' he said cheerfully over the sound of bikes being revved up and the beeps of alarms. They seemed to be rearranging the bikes and blokes were riding them up and down the aisles and around the outer walkway. 'They make it look so easy' I thought 'I'd be crashing into everything if I had to ride in such narrow spaces'. Dave told me the bike was just being checked over and asked me to come into his office and sort out the paperwork. As I handed over most of my life's savings Mike wandered off to look at the bikes. Once the paperwork was all done and dusted, and the logbook was in my hand, I looked at Dave and grinned. 'You'll love that little bike, I know you will but you'll be back for a bigger one' he said, echoing the words of the insurance girl. What was it with these people, size isn't everything. Dave showed me where to go to collect the bike and said it would be ready in about ten minutes. I went off to find Mike who had gone upstairs and was trying on a leather jacket. 'Why are you trying that on, you've already got a good biking jacket?' I asked him. 'I know but I fancy a leather one' he said as he wiggled his shoulders to adjust a waist length, bomber style jacket. I watched as he looked at himself in a long mirror, first straight on, then turning and looking over his shoulder then turning the other way and pulling the jacket tighter across his chest. What was he looking for? I suspect Steve McQueen from that film The Great Escape or someone like that anyway. 'C'mon' I said 'we haven't got time for this, the bike's nearly ready, we need to get going.'

Once Mike had collected his gear from the car, we made our way round to the service bay. There she stood, my Yamaha Virago 125cc, gleaming in the morning sunshine, a vision of beauty only slightly marred by the two L plates now sticking out from the front fork and hanging off the back number plate. I went over to stroke her and to let her know she was mine now. I know that sounds mad but motorbikes can affect you like that. The mechanic who had checked her over gave us the guided tour and explained all the controls and bits and pieces. I don't know why but I found myself apologising for her engine size. 'I know she's only little but I don't need anything powerful just yet' I said, somewhat pathetically. The mechanic, much to my surprise, said 'No, she's a nice piece of kit. I don't like bikes much myself. I only work here because I got made redundant from my last job and my brother works here and he got me in. Some of the big bikes are ridiculous if you ask me, they weigh a ton and I'm sure that half the blokes that ride 'em are scared of 'em but each to their own. I think this is a nice little bike.' I looked at Mike and grinned. Yes, this was my kind of biking conversation. Small is beautiful. Mike, however, was getting ready to ride it home and so chose not to respond. He sat on the bike, his long legs stretching forward nearly as far as the front wheel. Mike is six foot tall but he looked about nine foot tall sitting astride that little cruiser. He didn't look a happy man. I dashed back to the car, calling out as I went 'I'll set off and then wait for you' because I knew he wouldn't want me to watch him getting to grips with it. The last thing anybody wants is an audience at times like this. So I drove out of the car park and down the road a way, all the time checking my rear view mirror to see if he was following. I did catch a glimpse of him wobbling along so he was obviously on his way so I decided to press on and not put him off by dawdling just ahead of him. As I drove the next four or five miles I didn't see him again so I decided to wait in a lay by. Nothing. I waited and I waited and nothing. I began to panic. Where was he? Where was my bike? Surely there hadn't been an accident? That would be just my luck, bike and husband wiped out on first journey, I could just see the newspaper headlines. I was getting really anxious by now so decided to double back and try to find him. I got almost all the way back to the showroom when I spotted him at the side of the road. The bike was switched off and he was looking at the engine. 'Oh no' I thought 'I've only had it two minutes and it's broken down'. I pulled up behind him and jumped out. 'What's happened?' I yelled above the noise of the traffic. 'I don't know, it just packed up on me, the guy from the showroom is coming over in a minute' Mike said, looking like he could think of a million things he would rather be doing than this. Then the mechanic turned up. Without even looking at the bike he said 'It'll be the petrol, it'll need petrol. They come out with hardly any in the tank because it is too dangerous to have the showroom full of bikes that are full of petrol so they only put a tiny bit in. Switch it over to reserve and go straight to the petrol station down the road and you'll be okay'. I was annoyed, why didn't they tell us this when we left? How were we supposed to know that this was how things were done? When you get a new car they always fill it up with petrol for you so it seems logical to think they would do the same with a new bike. I decided not to say anything because I noticed that Mike was trying to act nonchalant about it all, to cover up the fact that he hadn't worked this out for himself. He switched the petrol tank over to reserve, started her up and set off. I drove along behind him to the first set of lights and then overtook him to give him a chance to ride the bike without towing an audience. Halfway home I pulled into a lay by to wait for him, just in case there had been anymore problems, but he tootled past me giving a thumbs up sign and I knew everything was now okay. He did look funny, this tall bloke on this little cruiser so unlike his own big monster bike. I thought he looked kinda cool, well that was until we got to a big hill just outside the town and his speed dropped and dropped until he was crawling along holding up everything behind him, including me. 'I wonder why he's going so slow' I thought, not realising that he was pushing the bike to it's limit, it being new and not run in at that stage. Finally he wobbled onto our drive, switched off the engine and kicked down the side stand. I parked on the road outside. 'Well?' I asked, full of excitement 'What's she like to ride?' Mike looked at the bike and then at me. 'Erm .. well .. it's quite a nice riding position, it feels relaxed and easy BUT ..' and it was a big but .. 'it's got no guts this bike'. My jaw dropped and the bubble of excitement that I had been living in for the last two hours, burst. 'No guts, what do you mean, no guts?' I spluttered angrily. Mike started laughing. 'Look, don't get mad at me, the bike's fine on the flat, a bit slow but okay, but get it on a hill and it just dies on you, it's just not powerful enough.' I studied his face carefully to see if he was joking. He wasn't joking. I felt hurt and betrayed - how dare he speak about my new bike like that, it was lovely. Mike must have seen how upset I was because he came over and put his arm round me and said 'Look, it isn't run in yet, it will probably go a bit faster once it's run in.' I looked at him, thinking 'more, say more things like that' and he did. With a little smile on his face he said 'It may not go very fast but I have to admit it's a great looking bike.' Didn't I tell you, he sometimes says just the right thing. Yes, it was a great looking bike and I was going to be a cool hen on a cool cruiser.

Staying close to home

In no way did it (the bike test) prepare me for the road.
Absolutely not. In the same way that sh***ing your girlfriend in a
Transit van does nothing to prepare you for married life.
Barry Sheene 1950 – 2003: The Biography by Stuart Baker

So now I had my lovely new bike but how was I going to learn
to ride it? I certainly wasn't going to take it out on the road
because, having had only about three hours of riding practice, I
knew I would be a danger to myself and every other road user
within half a mile of me. I knew I needed to practice off the road.
Opposite our house was an old school, which was turned into
council offices following some sort of education reorganisation a
few years ago. The school buildings became offices and the two
playgrounds, one at each end of the plot, became staff car parks.
The two playgrounds are linked by a narrow driveway that runs
both behind, and in front of, the building. That way if staff turn

up and find one car park is full they can drive round and try to find a place in the other. It was the perfect practice circle. 'Mike, I'm going to push the bike over the road and then ride it round the office car parks, now that most of the people have gone home' I told him, once we'd had a cup of tea. 'Pardon?' he said, looking at me like I had just spoken to him in a foreign language. I explained about the perfect practice circle. 'You don't need to do that, just get out on it and go for a ride for goodness sake' he said, shaking his head. 'I can't do that, I can't remember how to ride, I'll kill myself and then you'll be sorry' I wailed. He put his hands up and grinned 'Okay, okay .. if that is what you want to do, that's fine, you get on with it.' 'Just because he had hardly any practice and still managed to pass his test doesn't mean I can do that' I thought huffily. I decided to just ignore him and get on with my plan. So I put my old anorak on, got my helmet and gloves and went outside to get the bike and push it over the road. I pulled it up off it's side stand and started to try and manoeuvre it around to face the road. Gosh, it felt heavy. I decided to sit astride it and try to move it that way. That was a bit easier but it still felt very heavy. I began to doubt whether I could push it fast enough to get it over the road and into the car park before more traffic came along. Our road was a busy road. Oh, this was so frustrating. I glanced back at the house and saw that Mike was enjoying watching me struggle, from the front room window. I looked at him beseechingly and he looked back at me steadily, trying hard not to grin. I couldn't decide whether to laugh or scream. In the end I started laughing, but it was that sort of half laughing, half crying sort of laughing that happens when you find yourself in impossible situations. I heard the front door open and then shut and then Mike said 'C'mon, get off, I'll push it over for you' and he sat on it and without batting an eyelid, he sculled it over the road in about two seconds flat. I grabbed my helmet and gloves and ran over thinking 'It's not fair, I can't even move it when it's not switched on.' Mike jumped off the bike, kicked down the side stand and said 'There you go, it's all yours.' I wanted to get on it and ride off but it was on the narrow bit of the circle. 'Can you just take it round the corner, onto the car park bit, for me please' I whimpered pathetically. 'Maybe I should just ride it around for you as well?' he said as he sat back on it and sculled it round the corner and onto the car park. I thanked him and waited for him to leave. 'Go on then, let's see you ride it' he said. 'No, don't watch, you'll make me nervous, go back to the house' I whined. 'God, this is ridiculous' he said, but he turned on his heels and headed off back to the house.

So there I was, on my own, with my new bike. I glanced up at the office windows to check that no one was watching me. Mind you, what was I was going to do if anybody had been watching? Shout 'FIRE' perhaps, in an effort to clear the building but then, knowing my luck, the assembly point would be in the car park. Anyway, as luck would have it, no one was watching. I put my helmet and gloves on. Then I put the key in the ignition, sat on the bike, kicked up the side stand, switched on, checked the neutral light was on and pressed the starter button. The engine fired up first time. I felt the hairs stand up on the back of my neck. 'Here we go' I said to myself nervously and put the bike into first gear. I let out the clutch and gave it some revs and surged forward. It was like a repeat of my CBT session at the bike school. I kangarooed my way around the car park, which suddenly seemed very small. I rode round the front of the building in second gear, which I managed to get into when I remembered to flick the gear pedal up, and along the drive towards the bottom car park at the other

end. It was painfully slow and painfully fast all at the same time.
I tootled round the bottom car park, carefully avoiding the two or
three cars still parked there, and then went back along the drive
to the top car park. I repeated this circuit time after time. I also
practiced stopping by picking out a particular line on each car
park and then driving up to it to stop. At first I kept overshooting
the lines but then I managed to get it right after a while. After a
couple of hours of going round in circles I was exhausted so I
decided to go home. I managed to drive out of the car park, over
the road and into our drive, jerking to a stop by our garden gate.
I prized off my helmet and peeled off my gloves. I was hot and
sweaty. 'Phew, that was hard work' I said to Mike as he came out
to see how I'd got on. 'So, shall I get my bike out and we can go
out for a ride?' he said, full of eager anticipation. I just looked at
him. Was he kidding? I was exhausted and needed a sit down and
a cup of tea. He looked at me and realised that this was not going
to happen and, although I could see that he was disappointed, he
offered to take my bike round to the back of the house. 'Where
shall I put the bike?' he called back to me as he wrestled it
through the gate and down the path. 'On the patio' I said. He
stopped the bike and turned back towards me. 'What do you
mean on the patio, you said we couldn't keep bikes on the patio'.
I sighed. 'No, I said you couldn't keep your bike on the patio.'
I knew the minute that I said that I was asking for trouble but I
was so tired I wasn't as quick thinking as usual. 'Oh, so it's okay
to keep your bike on the patio, but not mine.' That was the last
thing I needed, a verbal jousting session with Mr Very Indignant.
'Look, your bike is on the path, there's nowhere else for mine
to go. Just put it on the patio for now and we can sort it out
later' I said, as I headed into the house to collapse on something
comfortable. Muttering to himself, he pushed it round the back

and propped it up outside the French windows, where it stayed, when I was not riding it, for several months until we bought a house with a garage!

Right bike, wrong house

You'll be the queen of the highway, my motorcycle mama.
Motorcycle Mama, Sailcat

Over the next few days this pattern of pushing my bike over the road, riding it round the car parks and riding it back across the road to get home, was repeated every evening when the council staff went home. I gradually got more confident and was able to get up to third gear on the drive between the top and bottom car parks. Also, the narrow driveway that ran round the back of the buildings was quite tricky to navigate having some tight bends, obstacles like huge dustbins and steps into some mobile huts located at the rear of the main building. I knew I was getting somewhere when I could ride right round the complete circuit using my first, second and third gears but then, just when I thought I might go out on the road I would chicken out and ride round the car parks again. Mike had given up on the idea of us going out together and had started going out on his own again, leaving me to go round in circles. Then one evening, when there seemed to be very little traffic about, I just came out of the car park, turned right and rode up to the traffic lights at the end of our road. 'Aaah, I'm on the road now, where shall I go' I thought, desperately trying to think of where the roads near us lead. I couldn't contemplate trying to turn right across oncoming traffic, it was just too difficult, so I turned left and set off towards the south end of the town. This road is fairly straight and although there is a roundabout about a quarter of a mile along it, it's a big one that you can go straight over without having to do any real cornering. I rode straight across. Scary stuff. Where now? I just kept going straight, which meant that I also had to go up the gears into fourth gear, which felt very daring. Fourth gear is such a long way from first gear if you have to stop. At the next junction the road forks so I took the left hand fork and rode down the hill towards a village on the outskirts of the town. Once in the village the road forks again and again I took the left hand fork that brought me round to another village. This time there was a T junction so I turned left. I was beginning to feel that I could handle turning left. The road I was on now is a long, winding road, with a steep hill at one end of it. I struggled up the hill in fourth gear as that was the gear I had been in when I got to the hill. It didn't occur to me to go down the gears to get more acceleration so I crawled up the hill praying that I would make it to the top. What an idiot. As I cleared the crest and started to pick up speed I felt so relieved. Now I was heading back towards the town and with just two more left turns to do I was home and wobbling onto the drive. I felt fantastic, and so triumphant, like I'd ridden across America or something.

Mike came through the gate having just parked his bike round the back on the patio. We were both using the patio as a car park now because, although I still didn't want to look out over a motorbike showroom forecourt, I couldn't bear the thought of putting my lovely machine out in the open on the garden path (our patio, being partly covered by an overhanging roof, provided a bit of shelter for anything stored close up to the French windows). Because I insisted on keeping my machine there I couldn't really make Mike put his on the path anymore and, in any case, my bike was so lovely to look at with all that chrome and soft leather that it didn't seem so bad having it blocking the view. 'Typical' said Mike when we first adopted this arrangement. 'When it's my bike, it's "You're not keeping it there" but now it's your bike it's suddenly okay.' What could I say? I decided to switch tack and get him focussed on something else other than my fickle views on bike parking. 'We need to buy a house with a garage, because over winter they will need to be garaged' This probably wasn't quite the right tack. 'Oh, so now you've got a lovely little Virago we have to move house!' he sneered. I realised I was going to have to move very slowly and carefully on this one. 'Well, we have been talking about getting another house, haven't we, but we just haven't got round to doing anything about it. Perhaps, now's a good time to have a look around and see what's out there' I said, in as soothing a tone as I could muster. He looked at me then shook his head and as he turned to leave the room I could here him chuckling to himself and saying 'You're a right one, you are.' I grinned secretly behind his back thinking 'Not a bad reaction, good, he'll go away and think about it now' and sure enough, he did. Five months later we moved into our new house around the corner with it's very own garage and our bikes, at last, had somewhere safe and dry to wile away the winter.

In the meantime I was getting on with getting out on the road. Just as I had spent days riding round the car park opposite, I now spent about a week riding round my left hand looping circle. Although this route was only about four miles long it had plenty of hazards to get to grips with – roundabouts, traffic lights, left turns, big main roads, country lanes, hills and bends and changing speed limits. Every time I wobbled back onto our drive I felt like I had just done a lap of the Isle of Man TT races, whatever they are. It was exhilarating. I always chose my time to go out very carefully and found that six o'clock in the evening was the best time because the rush hour traffic had gone and the roads were quiet before people started coming out for the evening. Nevertheless I still managed to make a real fool of myself on regular occasions. The thing I had most difficulty with was roundabouts. As I started to ride a bit faster I would find myself approaching roundabouts in third gear hoping they would be clear and I could keep going but then if I had to stop I was always in the wrong gear for starting off again. So I would then spend ages trying to get into first gear whilst the bike was at a stand still and, worrying about kangarooing off, I would also want to check it was in neutral before re engaging it in first gear. All this took time and the cars around me were probably fed up of waiting for me, though in fairness, none ever gave me any trouble. Thank goodness for L plates that's all I can say. I asked Mike what he did about gears at roundabouts. He looked at me with a thoughtful expression on his face and then said 'You knock down the gears as you approach the roundabout, you can do a few all at once, just keep knocking the gear pedal down.' What was he saying? 'No, you need to go down the gears one at a time as you slow down, don't you, and sometimes I haven't got enough road left to go down a gear, ride a bit, go down another gear and so on' I moaned. He snorted with laughter. 'You don't do that, just knock the gears down, however many you need to knock down, one after the other'. Really, was it that simple? Next time out I tried this and lo and behold, I could knock the bike down to first gear in the last few feet of road if it became clear that I was going to have to stop. It was a fantastic feeling being able to drive towards junctions and not have to stop at them all. The other thing I had a problem with was going round the tight left hand corner at the lights at the end of our road. If I was first at the lights this meant I had to set off and turn left after a few feet. This combination of riding and steering meant that I usually ground round in first gear, not having the skill to ride, corner and change gear all at once. My little bike was much better in second gear when trundling along slowly. I hated being first at the line and sometimes, if I could see a car behind me on the road leading up to the lights, I would pull over and let them pass just so I could be behind them at the lights. This would then give me enough room to set off, change gear and then steer round the corner. If I did go a bit faster I always ended up going wide round the corner with the result that I found myself more than once, peering almost into the lap of the driver waiting on the other side of the road to turn right. Still, by choosing my riding times carefully I was only coping with very light traffic. I slowly began to feel more confident, which was just as well because Mike was keen for us to go out on a little ride together. 'Maybe when he sees how slow and clumsy I am on the open road he won't be so keen anymore' I thought.

Riding the Dales

*You and me, we'll go motorbike ridin' in the sun and the wind and
the rain*
*I go money in my pocket, got a tiger in my tank, And I'm king of
the road again*
Jeans on. David Dundas

It was a lovely sunny morning when we took our first ride out
together. 'We won't go far' Mike said, 'We'll follow your left
hand loop but instead of turning left in the village we'll go
straight on across country to the next town and then loop back in
a bigger circle. Do you think you can manage that?' He gave me
his cautious optimist look. 'Do I think I can manage that? I've no
idea' I thought but said 'Yes, of course, that'll be fine.' We got our
helmets and gloves and wrestled the bikes out onto the drive. 'Do
you need petrol?' Mike asked. I looked in the tank and there was
petrol in it so I said no. I wasn't worried because I knew there

was also a reserve petrol tank somewhere on the bike because Mike had had to switch over to that on his way back from the showroom, so even if I did run out I could always switch over and start using that tank till I could get to a petrol station. I wondered where that tank was, probably behind one of these round bits at the side. The whole bike engine thing was a complete mystery to me. I had no idea what any of the bits were apart from the main petrol tank and I knew how to check the oil through the little glass disk near the bottom of the engine and the brake fluid through the little glass disk on the box on the handlebars. Apart from that it was all just machinery to me.

We set off, Mike leading and me behind. It was great to be following him, after all that was the reason I had learnt to ride in the first place, so that we could go out together. I got round the horrible lights okay and over the big roundabout and then started my slow ascent up the first big hill. Mike just sailed away in front of me. I couldn't believe it. He looked like he was riding on the flat as his Honda just loped off into the distance. By now I had realised that the best way to go up hills was to go down the gears so I dropped down to a lower gear and started trying to race after him. No such luck, even in the lower gear I was chuntering up the hill. 'So much for riding out together' I thought to myself as I scanned the horizon to see if I could see him. 'It's a good job we agreed the route beforehand' I mumbled to myself just before I spotted him waiting for me in a lay by. I pulled in behind him, beaming with pleasure and giving him the thumbs up sign. He nodded and pulled off again with me following on behind. Everything was fine as we stuck to the speed limits through the town and the outlying villages but once we hit the open road he was off again and nowhere to be seen. At first I felt a bit sorry for myself . 'Why doesn't he wait for me, we're supposed to be riding together' a little voice whined in my head, but then I just thought 'Oh shut up whinging and just enjoy yourself, you're doing fine and this is good fun'. So that is what I did. I kept catching up with him at junctions and through villages and then he would zoom off again. About two thirds of the way round Mike pulled into a lay by and we both had a drink of water from a bottle in his rucksack. 'Look, if we get split up on the way back, you just head off home and I'll see you there. I know my way back' I said. Mike looked at me with a 'Does she really mean that?' look on his face. We have had those conversations in the past, like I imagine most couples have, which run along the lines of 'Well I know I said that but I didn't think you would actually do it' (me speaking) followed by 'Why did you say it, if you didn't want me to do it' (Mike speaking), followed by 'Well I thought you'd realise that although I said that I didn't mean you to do it' and so on. I try not to have conversations like this now having learnt that men and subtle mind games don't mix that well and it's better, as they say in Yorkshire to, 'call a spade a spade' and have done with it. So I said 'Honestly, that's fine, you get off and I will see you back at the ranch.' With a big grin on his face he hopped on his bike and was soon sailing away into the distance. I cruised along. Yes, I was cruising in the morning sunshine thinking that this really was great fun. Then just on the outskirts of the town my bike started to lose speed dramatically. It wasn't on a hill so it shouldn't have been doing that. I dropped the gears and it picked up slightly but then fizzled out again, coming to a complete stop by the side of the road. 'What the …?' I thought. Then I began telling myself not to panic. I was okay, I had pulled in to the side of the road, it was only a motorbike, the worst that could happen is that it would need to be towed (towed?) home. I looked around me and saw, on the opposite side of the road, the entrance to the police traffic headquarters for the area. The place where all the cop cars and police motorcycles hang out when they are not rushing off to scenes of crime or accidents or stalking speeding road users. 'Oh great' I thought 'any minute now I am going to be surrounded by helpful policeman asking me what's wrong and why have I stopped right opposite a driveway, their driveway as a matter of fact, and was this my machine?'. I had visions of my complete ignorance about motorbikes becoming obvious within thirty seconds of me opening my mouth and they would then have to confiscate my bike to protect me from myself, and my silly dream of being a cool hen on a cool cruiser. So, expecting the worst, I waited for a gap in the traffic and then pushed the bike over the road and onto the edge of their drive to get me off the road and give me a bit of time to work out what to do next. I looked at the bike. What was wrong with it? I opened the petrol tank and looked inside. There was still petrol in there. I checked the oil window, which was pointless as the oil was all running round the engine and nowhere to be seen. I panicked, where was the oil? Then I remembered about waiting for it to settle before checking it. I told myself to stay calm. 'Please don't do this to me, I don't know hardly anything about bikes but I do love you and I promise I will look after you and cherish you if you start again and just take me home' I pleaded with the bike. I pressed the starter button. Nothing. I tried again. Nothing. 'You sod!' I yelled at it. What to do now? I fished my mobile phone out of my jacket and switched it on. It bleeped almost immediately with an answerphone message. I listened. It was Mike sounding worried 'Where are you? You should be back by now. Ring me.' What a funny thing to ask, because, if I had been in an accident, whipping out my mobile phone to tell him would probably be the last thing on my mind as I lay splattered on the road. It was nice to hear his voice though so I immediately returned the call to get his help and ask him what to do next. 'What's happened, where are you?' he said, sounding very worried now. I explained about the bike dying on me and Mike said it had been like that when he was riding back from the showroom. He thought it would be the petrol. 'Switch it over to the reserve tank' he said. 'But there is petrol in the tank, I can see it, it's not that' I said, but as I said this I switched it over just to see how to do it. I tried to start it again. Nothing. So I switched it back in case I flooded the engine. I wasn't sure if you could flood a motorbike engine and I didn't even know what that meant in the car but I do remember when I was driving old bangers that if they wouldn't start you had to be careful not to give them too much choke or press down the accelerator too much in case you flooded the engine. Could you do that with the bike? I pressed the starter button again more out of anger than anything else and the bike started up. I couldn't believe it. I shouted to Mike on the phone, 'It's going, I am going to try and get home, see you in a minute'. I jumped on the bike and eased it around onto the road and trundled the remaining half a mile home.

Mike was pacing up and down the drive, watching for me with a worried look on his face which turned into a huge smile as I chugged round the corner and finally wobbled onto the drive. 'You made it then, is the bike alright now or what?' he asked me as I struggled to remove my helmet and gloves which were both sticky and sweaty from the long ride, especially the last stressed out half a mile of it. 'I don't know but I'm ringing the garage. I've only had it a couple of weeks and it's breaking down. They need to come and look at it' I said wearily, still angry about what had

happened but also relieved to be home. I rang the garage. 'It'll be
the petrol, it sounds like it needs petrol' said the man on the other
end of the line. 'No, it's not that' I say ' there's petrol in the tank'
and after a short discussion in which it must have become obvious
to the man at the garage that he was talking to a mechanical half
wit, he agreed to get the mechanic, who was out delivering bikes,
to call on his way back from his last drop. About two hours later
the doorbell rang and I opened the door to find a huge van on
the drive and a big friendly man wearing blue overalls. 'Are you
Jackie?' he asked me with a smile. I said 'Yes' and then showed
him the bike and told him what had happened. He looked at the
bike and then asked me for the key and opened the petrol tank.
'You need petrol, that's all' he said. I started to explain that that
couldn't be right (as if I'd know) and that there was petrol in the
tank, you could see it. He said 'Yes that's the reserve petrol; it's
all in the same tank. There isn't a special reserve tank or anything
but you'd know that anyway from reading your manual, wouldn't
you. If you flick the tank switch over to reserve it will get you
to the petrol station and you can fill up. You say you switched it
over temporarily when you came to a stop, well that's probably
how you got home, it let just enough fuel through for you to get
home.' It was one of those 'God I wish the earth would open
and swallow me up' moments. A few months later I read that
the same thing had happened to Robert Pirsig, famous author
of Zen and the Art of Motorcycle Maintenance, who abandoned
a planned holiday and had to switch to the car when his bike
seemingly broke down. He wrote: 'Two weeks after the vacation
was over, one evening after work, I removed the carburettor to
see what was wrong but still couldn't find anything. To clean
off the grease before replacing it, I turned the stopcock on the
tank for a little gas. Nothing came out. The tank was out of gas.

I couldn't believe it. I can still hardly believe it. I have kicked myself mentally a hundred times for that stupidity and don't think I'll ever really, finally get over it. Evidently what I saw sloshing around was gas in the reserve tank which I had never turned on. I didn't check it carefully because I assumed the rain had caused the engine failure. I didn't understand then how foolish quick assumptions like that are.' So I now know it can happen to the most mechanically minded of people never mind complete no hopers like me but that was no comfort to me then as I stood there blushing to my roots. Mike was nowhere to be seen. I must have looked really pathetic because the mechanic then seemed to take pity on me and talked me all through the bike and its controls again. He even asked me to get the manual so he could show me which pages to look at for things like tyre pressures. When I brought the manual out it was written in German! The mechanic then took even more pity on me and started to have a moan about the sales people back at the garage. 'They should have given you an English version, how the hell are you supposed to be able to read that. No wonder you couldn't make head nor tail of this stuff.' I said 'Yes, that's right they should have given me an English one' as if that explained everything, when in fact I hadn't even looked at the manual and probably wouldn't have done even if it had been in English. 'Ring them up and get them to send you an English one' he said, smiling. He really was very nice and making light of my stupidity. I said I was sorry to have dragged him all the way out for something so trivial. He said he was passing anyway and not to worry he had had worse call outs than this. 'Like what?' I said, thinking it might make me feel better to hear about other people's stupid mistakes. 'Oh, I've had people who say their bike keeps stalling for no reason and it's because they always set off with the side stand down, which cuts out the engine, and others say it won't go at all and it's because they've accidentally knocked the emergency off switch which cuts out the engine entirely and, well you name it we've had it.' I rolled my eyes in mock disbelief but all the time listening intently and cataloguing each error for future reference, vowing to myself I would try to remember not to do any of these things. Just as the man was about to leave Mike sauntered out and said 'Hi, what's the problem then?' The man explained about the petrol. Mike nodded sagely and said 'I said it was that' and then looked at me and then at the man with one of those 'She wouldn't listen to me mate' looks on his face and the mechanic smiled and nodded back at him with one of those 'I know what you mean mate, women eh?' looks on his face. I bit my lip, forced a smile and went inside to ring my insurers and get Roadside Breakdown Assistance added to my bike insurance policy.

The secret world of biking

There's something about riding a bike – the concentration and single-mindedness of it, and the desire to get it right, taking a corner fast without losing control, doing it beautifully, getting into a groove and winning the battle between your head telling you to do one thing, the bike wanting to do another and your body in between – that I miss like hell if I don't get to ride it every day. I walk into the house and I'm chilled.
Ewan McGregor: Long Way Round, Chasing shadows across the world.

Over the next few weeks, as I continued to go out on my bike, sometimes on my own and sometimes with Mike, I slowly came to realise that the world of biking is all around us but hidden just below the surface until you know how to see it. By riding my bike, I began to connect with this parallel biking universe. I first became aware of it when, out on my own, a bike passed me and the rider nodded his head at me. It took me by surprise. Did I know him? Was it Tim the builder who I knew had a motorbike but I couldn't remember what make. Perhaps it was him and he was doing the biking equivalent of waving. Then it happened again, and again. All these bikes were whizzing past me on my little Virago – big cruisers, flashy sports bikes and stately tourers – and all the riders were giving me a friendly nod. I asked Mike what it was all about. He explained that it is just something that most bikers do. 'It is sort of like a 'Welcome to the Biking Fraternity' nod. How wonderful. I felt like I had been given membership of St Andrews Golf club when all I could play was pitch and putt. So I began to nod back. Occasionally a biker, usually on a particularly aggressive looking speed bike, wouldn't nod so I would nod first and then if they didn't nod back I would feel embarrassed thinking they were probably wondering who the nut on the 125 was, nodding at them on their supreme machine. I also nodded at scooters until Mike pointed out that they are not usually included in this particular ritual. 'Why not?' I said, jumping to the defence of scooter lovers the world over. 'I don't know, they just don't seem to be included, that's all, and they don't usually nod back if you notice' said Mike a bit defensively. I began to watch scooters carefully and I have to say that quite a few of the ones I nodded at, did nod back so maybe they did want to be included. I committed myself to nodding at everyone on two motorised wheels. I know this sounds mad but it did feel nice to be nodded at and it did make me feel a bit like a cool hen on a cool cruiser after all.

The other place where the biking parallel universe seemed to rise to the surface was in the house whenever we had to call anyone in to do building work or repairs to main services or electrical appliances. One minute we would have the dishwasher repairman kneeling on our kitchen floor and the next minute we'd have mad Barry the biker. Since we took up biking, nearly every bloke that has come to the house to do any sort of practical job has turned out to be a biker. If they come through the front door and catch a glimpse of the bikes through the French windows on the patio, they are off. The kettle goes on and we spend the next hour talking about bikes, thoughts on different makes, interesting journeys and good places to ride to, prices of bikes and where to buy them, accidents that can and have happened, mishaps and funny stories and, well you name it and we end up talking about it. Even with our small business it turns out that many of the people we deal with ride bikes or have ridden bikes in the past. Business meetings take ages because the biking agenda takes up the first hour or so and then the rest of the actual work has to be squashed into the last ten minutes. Visits to the house, because we work from home, almost always include a guided tour of the bikes and, much to Mike's annoyance, usually revolves around a quick look at his and a long perusal of mine. Comments like 'It looks bigger than a 125cc' and 'Very smart looking' fly around all over, whilst I glow with pride and pleasure and give Mike my 'See, they think my bike is better than yours' look. Of course, he then has to chip in and say things like 'Yes, it's nice looking but it is absolutely hopeless on the hills' and 'Because it's so big it's very heavy for a 125 so that obviously slows it down'. Then a discussion about bhp's and torque and other such stuff ensues and I have to look on, nod and act like I know what they are talking about.

Also, once people know you've got a motorbike they start turning up on theirs. Any excuse to hop onto two wheels instead of into four. When we moved to the new house it needed a lot of work doing on it so we contacted Tim our builder and asked him to come round and give us a quote. He turned up on his red Triumph Speed Triple and spent about fifteen minutes looking over the house and about 45 minutes showing Mike all around the bike. Bikers are also good at coming up with reasons for why they need to nip out on the bike. The best excuse I ever heard was from Tim again. He and his wife own a caravan about 90 miles away from home and, after having driven down there one weekend, he realised they had left a carton of milk in the fridge. 'Well, it's obviously going to go off and stink the place out so I told the missus I needed to pop down there and chuck it out' he said, grinning mischievously. Not bad, eh? A 180 mile round trip to throw out a carton of milk. Good one.

The last time I went to the hairdressers I had to go on my motorbike. My hairdresser owns two shops, one just down the road from our house and one 20 miles away. When he first opened the new shop about 6 months ago he didn't have many customers so it was a lot easier to get an appointment there. As I always think to get my hair cut when it is about three weeks longer than it should be, I always want an appointment at short notice and, well, it's easier to get an appointment at short notice at the salon that just happens to be 20 miles away. That's my excuse anyway. When I told all this to Joel he laughed and said 'Well it's funny you should say that. I've got three biking customers who live near you and they all come here for their hair cutting and they all come on their bikes'. As he said this I could see him looking sadly at my hair, which looked a bit like something you might get if you styled a scarecrow with brylcream. It has to be said that motorbike helmets play havoc with your hair, which is probably why lots of bikers have shaved heads or very short hair or very long hair that can be pulled back into a pony tail. Any other style doesn't stand a chance. No matter how much gel, hair spray, wax or whatever you use to try to keep your hair looking good, the minute you put on that helmet your hair is doomed. 'Joel, can you cut my hair so that it looks good when I take my helmet off?' I asked him, a look of complete faith on my face as he really is an excellent hairdresser. His shoulders sagged. 'Well that all depends upon how much you love your biking' he replied, lifting up my soggy locks and watching them flop back flat onto my head. 'What do you mean?' I said. 'The only cut I can give you that will look the same before and after you wear a helmet is a number two cut' he said in a serious voice. I studied his face carefully. Was he serious? Shave my head? It must have been the shocked look on my face that forced him to let out the laugh that he had obviously been working hard to suppress. 'All you bikers ask me this and it can't be done. You have to accept that if you ride bikes you'll have helmet hair' he said matter of factly. 'Oh well, just do it as short as you can without making me look like a bloke' I said, all dreams of a stylish, short Annie Lennox type cut gone. In fact, one of the first things to go when you get into biking is any hairstyle with bounce, spikes or fluffy curls. Helmets just don't let you do bounce. Instead you have to resign yourself to the flat, sweaty, stuck to your head look, which is why you need a really sexy bike, so that people look at that and not at you.

Right bike, wrong clothing

In the twenty-first century motorcycle racing is one of the most colourful sports on the calendar, but it wasn't always the case, far from it in fact, and Sheene played a large part in the technicolour transformation. In 1972 he ordered a set of white leathers, again largely as a gimmick to get noticed but also as a way of improving the sport's then drab, greasy image of rough men in black leathers riding noisy, smelly motorbikes....Sheene would later ditch the white colour scheme believing it was a step too far, but he would go on to wear other brightly coloured leathers such as the famous blue and white Suzuki garments and the even more famous red and black Texaco outfit.
Barry Sheene 1950 – 2003: The Biography by Stuart Barker

After I had had the bike for a few weeks I decided that I needed a decent biking jacket. I was tired of wearing big jumpers under my oversized anorak so we headed back up to the bike school to look at their selection. Mike had a black and blue jacket so I knew that I had to steer clear of blue. The idea that people might think that we were deliberately wearing matching gear made me shudder. How could I be a cool hen if people were saying things like 'Oh how cute, matching gear for Mr and Mrs Biker'. I didn't want people to think I was only getting into biking because my husband wanted me to, even though it was true. No, I wanted to be seen as a biker in my own right and that meant wearing different gear. I love the colour blue though and as I looked through the alternatives I began to resent the fact that he had taken that colour. 'Why did you have to pick blue for your jacket?' I asked him peevishly. He looked slightly confused. 'I like blue' he said, 'What's wrong with blue?' I lifted down a yellow and black jacket and looked at it half heartedly. 'Nothing is wrong with blue, but I like blue.' Now looking very confused, he said 'So get a blue jacket, what's the problem?' I put the yellow and black one back and turned towards the all in one suits. 'I can't get blue, can I, because you've got blue and people might think we are trying to colour co-ordinate or something.' Mike looked at me with his 'You are joking, aren't you' expression on his face then seeing that I wasn't he just shrugged his shoulders and said 'Whatever'. I hate that word. How can you have a good argument when your opponent adopts the verbal equivalent of playing dead? As he wondered off to look at the boots I decided to try on a black and red jacket. Red isn't really my colour but I didn't fancy any of the other combinations.

Biking gear is fascinating in that its primary purpose is to protect you from any cold, wet weather you might ride in and any hard road or other surfaces you might fall or get thrown on. This means it has to be made of waterproof material (unless you go for leather which looks great but soaks up water like a sponge apparently) and have lots of zips and Velcro straps to keep it fastened tight to your body. It also has to be thick and padded and have protective pads in key places like over your spine, around your shoulders and over your elbows. Once you get fastened into your gear it feels a bit like a slightly flexible coat of armour. As I zipped myself into the jacket I began to feel a bit like C-3PO, the robot, in Star Wars. As I waddled over to the mirror to take a look I felt like saying 'Master, I really must complain about this clothing ..'. I suppose it didn't look too bad, it was just choking me a bit round the neck. Danny came over to take a look. 'You know, we've got the trousers to go with that and they are on special offer at the moment. If you buy the jacket you get 50% off the trousers.' I looked at Danny and said 'You don't really need trouser though do you?' He shook his head and, as he lifted a pair down from the rack, said 'No but they're a damn site warmer than jeans when the weather gets a bit colder and they give you a lot more protection. Here, why not try some on. What size are you, about a 12?' I went all soft and agreeable. I hadn't been a size 12 in years so it was wonderful to hear someone say those few kind words. Mike snorted from where he was standing further down the aisle. 'A size 12, hardly .. more like a 16 if you ask me.' I looked at him daggers. We weren't asking him, were we? Anyway I was a small 16, maybe even a large 14. Danny grinned and pointed to the rack and said 'Just help yourself Jackie, I'm sure you'll find your size.' That rat Mike, I'd have a few words to say to him when we got home.

So I chose some medium trousers and, in the changing room that was a tiny space behind a narrow curtain in the corner, I struggled to get into them. This was not because they were too small but because they were thick, stiff and padded in various places with hard plastic protector pads. I finally managed to get them on and waddled out of the changing corner. I felt a bit like Wallace in the wrong trousers. Motor bike gear makes real sense when you are riding around on your motorbike but when you are standing looking at yourself in a shop mirror it looks very bulky, sort of astronaut style. For one thing, because your knees are bent on the motorbike the trousers ride up, so the kneepads are fixed in lower down. This means that when you are standing up they are like hockey shin pads that bulge out about half way down your shins. The jackets and trousers are also quilted to keep you warm which translates into keep you sweaty when they are not being air cooled by winds of up to, in my case, about 50 miles an hour. I asked Mike what he thought. 'They look fine to me, anyway it's not up to me, you decide, if you like them, get them' he said, only half looking my way because by now he was trying on some boots. It crossed my mind to point out that he had hardly looked at me and how was I supposed to get a proper opinion from him when he was obviously not going to give this matter much attention but then I decided against it. I have never been much good at choosing clothes and regularly wear slightly peculiar combinations and outfits to which Mike says things like 'What are you wearing?' and 'You're not wearing that with those are you?' When I retort with 'What do you mean? They look fine' he just says 'Okay' and never makes a big fuss about my nonexistent dress sense. I hate to admit it but he might be right about my choice of outfits because my daughter Helen frequently echos his sentiments, but much more vociferously, saying things like 'I'm not going out with you if you're wearing that!' and 'Mum, that looks terrible, go and put that other one on, you know, the one that I said looked okay last week.' At times like these Mike's gentle admonishments seem positively supportive in comparison so I thought it probably wasn't a good idea to alienate my one ally against the fashion police over a debate about motorbike gear. The jacket and trousers were okay so I decided to buy them.

I did spend a bit of time looking at the all-in-one outfits but just couldn't see myself in one of those and 'In any case', I thought, 'it must be murder when you want to go to the loo, you must practically have to strip naked to use the toilet'. The all-in-one outfits remind me of the babygrows my girls used to wear as babies but much tighter and more garish and, it seems to me, they are mainly worn by the speed bikers. I couldn't imagine a Harley rider being seen dead in one, if you'll excuse the phrase. Many of these outfits are decorated with great stripes and zig zigs and as they flash past I often imagine that the wearers must think of themselves as the sort of X Men of the road. Once when I was waiting at the traffic lights at the crematorium on the edge of town, a speed bike came round the corner and when the rider saw my little cruiser he revved up his bike and reared the front end up into the air to do, what I believe is called, a 'wheelie'. I was shocked. Why was he doing that? How dangerous, and right outside the crematorium, it seemed almost disrespectful. He, and I'm assuming it was a he, well either that or she was a very flat chested female, was wearing one of these leather babygrows. It was a lime green colour, with various garish markings and it looked like it had been sprayed on his body. As he stood there doing his Lone Ranger – Hi Ho, Silver Away impression it suddenly came to me that he looked a bit like Kermit the frog and I just had to smile. The latest craze seems to be having some sort of ears on your helmet and it is not unusual to see these X Men in the leather babygrows with helmet bunny ears, very strange. Perhaps they are trying to tell us that they are very fast and dangerous but a bit cuddly too. Mind you, at least you don't have to grow a beard to be a speed biker. If, on the other hand, you fancy cruising around on a Harley Davidson, it seems almost compulsory to have a beard and not just a short, close cropped neat little beard but quite a long straggly one and preferably grey. Long hair and ponytails seem to be part of that scene as well. The touring bikers on the other hand, on the big bikes that look like armchairs with small fridges bolted on the back, always look cool and sensible as they glide past in black leather with matching helmets sporting intercom microphones. Of course, I generalise but I've seen these stereotypes often enough to make me wonder if each type of bike comes with a secret dress code. At that stage, I was still trying to work out the dress code for cool hens on cool cruisers and the only thing I was certain about was that didn't include beards!

By this time, Mike had decided to get himself a pair of boots. Danny popped up again and said 'I'll do you a deal. Buy two pairs of these same boots and I'll let you have the second pair at a discounted rate'. What is this, milk the punters week? Mike said to me 'You could do with a pair of boots, why don't you try some of these on' and that is how we managed to go home that day ladened down with a new jacket and trousers for me and two pairs of, what I can only describe as, Captain America boots. The only thing missing now was a pair of trousers for Mike and these he bought a few weeks later from the place where I had bought the motorbike. He chose tight black leather and, in spite of all his grinning and winking and murmerings of 'ooh, black leather trousers', when he wears them he definitely looks like he's got frogs legs.

Me on my dad's scooter

Me, my sister and friend in the open top sidecar

My nana and grandad and aunty Dora posing for a family
photograph

Mike's first bike - a Honda

My lovely little Yamaha Virago 125 cc cruiser

My mum on her Honda 90 with the basket on the back

Riding in the dales on the Yamaha and Honda

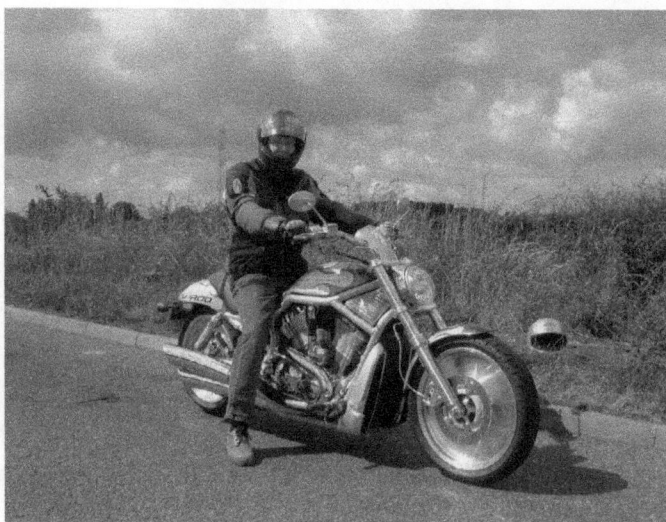

Mike test riding the Harley Davidson V Rod

Mike's V Rod - a sensation on wheels

A hog and a hen at a family pit stop

Bike for sale

Bella joins the family

Living with 2 Harleys

Riding the dales on our Harleys

Big Yamaha meets little Yamaha

In a car you're always in a compartment, and ...everything you
see is just ... moving by you boringly in a frame. On a cycle the
frame is gone. You're completely in contact with it all. You're in
the scene, not just watching it anymore and the sense of presence
is overwhelming... you spend your time being aware of things and
meditating on them.
Zen and the Art of Motorcycle Maintenance – Robert M Pirsig

Now that we had the proper gear we were keen to be a bit more
adventurous so we started looking for places to go that were
further afield. We live in the Midlands and so are lucky to have
some interesting countryside all around us but we quickly found
that our favourite rides were up in the Derbyshire Dales. We
would get up quite early on sunny weekend mornings and look
at each other and say 'Get the bikes out!' then get ready and head

off to the Dales, usually to Ashbourne where we would stop for a coffee. This raised the problem of securing the bikes. Mike wasn't too worried and seemed happy to just park up and leave his but I, on the other hand, was semi paranoid about someone stealing my dream machine. 'How do you lock them?' I asked Mike. He thought for a minute and then said 'Well you've got a number of options. You can either buy a big chain and then chain it to something or you could pay a bit for it to be alarmed or you could buy a disk lock'. He explained that a disk lock was a small lock that fastened onto the brake disk on the front wheel to stop the wheel going round, so this should stop anyone trying to wheel your bike away. I didn't fancy a chain as I had seen people riding with these looped over their shoulders like bandits bullet belts and I didn't want something that heavy digging into my shoulder. Plus, I didn't have any panniers or a top box to carry luggage so whatever I bought needed to be highly portable. The disk lock is small enough to carry in a pocket but disabling enough to act as a deterrent. Mike told me not to worry because no one was going to be interested in nicking a 125cc but I was not so sure. He could be all relaxed about this sort of thing because, if the truth be known, he didn't really love his machine but I loved mine and couldn't bear the thought of coming out of a café and finding it gone. Besides which, it looked bigger than a 125cc so they might nick it thinking it was a bigger bike. 'I think bike thieves can tell what size engine a bike has, I imagine they are quite experts in bikes and which makes are which' he said, with his 'Oh you do like to worry unnecessarily' look on his face. I chose to ignore that and went off to buy a disk lock from the local bike shop.

Whilst I was at the shop I got some visor cleaning spray too. I am always surprised by how mucky your visor can get. The worst mess is when a bluebottle hits you at high speed and explodes like a small custard bomb, splattering your mini windscreen and ruining the view. Sometimes a fly hits and sticks but doesn't splatter and then it is really difficult not to go cross eyed trying to look at it instead of the road ahead. Bees are so big that when they hit your visor they make a loud bang and you nearly jump off your seat. In very warm weather I like to ride with the visor up but then the flies hit you right in the face which stings a bit. Still it is not too bad if you wear sunglasses, at least the flies don't get in your eyes then. I used to worry about getting a wasp or a bee in my helmet but one of the biking magazines gave a good bit of advice which said that if that happens, do a lifesaver look over your shoulder and the wasp will hopefully get blown out of your helmet again. I haven't had to do it yet but hopefully this tactic will work if and when I do. I also learnt very early on not to try and wipe my visor clean whilst travelling along because the result usually looked something like my youngest daughter's high chair tray when she was a baby and tipped her baby food into it and swirled it all around with her fingers. Better instead to just ignore the splats and smudges until I got back home and could give my visor a proper clean.

So, in our new biking gear, with clean visors and a disk lock in my pocket, off we would go riding the thirty or so miles to Ashbourne. For Mike, this often involved waiting for me to catch him up but not by much as there is a big hill just outside Ashbourne and usually I could get up some speed coming down that and close the gap enough to time my arrival not long after his. Unfortunately, this had the opposite effect on the way home when I would take forever to struggle up this hill and another just on the outskirts of our town and he would be home, out of his gear and drinking a cup of tea by the time I got back in. Still it didn't matter so much on the way home. Once in Ashbourne, we would park up, lock up and go for a coffee. It was good fun and I always felt a bit giddy with the thrill of it all. We would then stroll round the antique shops and book shops, or rather waddle round them in our padded biking gear before getting back on the bikes and riding home. The only problem I kept having was forgetting to take off my disk lock. I would sit on the bike, flick up the side stand, start the engine and then try to roll it forward to get into a good position for moving off. Then it would get stuck. At first I thought I had done something wrong with the gears and would spend ages putting the bike into neutral and then into gear and then trying to roll it forward again. It took me a while to twig that the disk lock was still on. I would then have to switch the bike off, flick down the side stand, get off and remove the disk lock. I hate to admit it but I kept doing this, once nearly falling off the bike outside Mike's sister's house. There I was, trying to look all cool and confident but as I pushed the bike forward energetically, it slammed to a halt with me nearly going over the handlebars. Talk about uncool. Then one day I was in the local petrol station and noticed that one of the biking magazines had a free gift on the front called a disk lock reminder. It was a bright lime green coiled stretchy thing with a key ring loop at one end and a loop of cord at the other. The key ring loop fits over your disk lock and then you have to stretch the coil and loop the other end over your handlebar. In fact, reading the article about the free gift and why they had included it, I learnt that my experiences were fairly trivial. Some bikers have tried to ride off at speed and ended up with damaged brake calipers, cracked mudguards, scratched wheel forks and twisted brake disks. Others ended up dropping their bikes causing all sorts of damage and in some cases, the riders and their pillion passengers were badly hurt as bikes fell over or collar bones were broken when their shoulders were badly jarred as their bikes hit the kerb. So in spite of the fact that when it is in place my bike looks like it is being attacked by a bright green slinky, I started to use it all the time and never forgot to take the disk lock off again.

Sometimes we would press on to Carsington Reservoir, which has a big visitors centre with nice toilets and a good coffee shop. The first time we went there, we pulled into the car park and looked for somewhere to park. There was a section for bikes so we parked in that. Just as I was switching off my bike an enormous Yamaha pulled up at the side of me with a huge man in black leathers sitting astride it. I don't know what particular model his bike was but it was about 1100cc. It looked massive. It was like the motorbike equivalent of a shire horse being tethered up next to a Shetland pony. I gave him a weak smile as he tugged off his helmet. 'Cor, that's a bit of a daddy bear bike compared to my little tidger' I said, trying not to look too intimidated. The rider, who was about 6 foot 5 with a barrel for a chest, looked at me and said 'That's a little Virago isn't it? They're nice little bikes those. My mate has got a 535 Virago and he swears by it, he loves it, says it's one of the best cruisers ever made'. My heart sang. What a nice man. Mike started chatting to him about the big Yamaha whilst I fiddled with the disk lock and reminder thing. We asked him what happened about getting a car park ticket. He explained that bikes were exempt because where were you supposed to put a ticket? Even if you bought one it would probably blow off or some other driver could just take it. I hadn't thought of that. Usually we park on the roadside where limited parking is allowed or go to places where parking is free so this was a new thing to think about. We took his advice and left the bikes and went and got a coffee but all the time I was worrying about whether we did need a parking ticket or not. 'You're such a worry wart, just forget about it and come and look at the views over the reservoir. It's lovely out here and the yachts are all out on the water now' said Mike, using his 'lets divert her onto something else' tack which he has mastered over the years as a way to get my mind off something that is niggling me.

Early one sunny morning in late autumn, we set off and rode to Ashbourne. It was so early that the coffee shops weren't open so we pressed on to Parsley Hay. This is a small rest place at the top of the Tissington Trail and we often stop there for a cup of tea when we come to the Dales to cycle in the summer, before riding our bicycles back down the trail to Ashbourne. The views from this point are fantastic and it really is a lovely place to break a journey whether on bicycles or motorbikes. Unfortunately, the food kiosk here was also shut. By now the sun had gone in and we were feeling the cold. Having set off in sunshine, and being inexperienced about riding later in the year, we never thought we would get cold. I was wearing my full space man suit so wasn't too bad but Mike was wearing jeans and his legs were cold. Also, our hands were freezing in thin summer gloves. We pushed on to Buxton and again found nowhere open where we could get a hot drink and warm up a bit. We managed to find a public loo and use that and then set off over the tops to Leek. The road between Buxton and Leek has some spectacular views and the sun came out again as we rode up, or in my case struggled up, and around the edge of the Roaches and then dropped down into Leek. The ride down was exhilarating and I found myself laughing out loud and shouting 'Yee hi' in my helmet. I know, it's a form of biking madness. Once in Leek we decided to press on home. Having covered about 90 miles almost non stop, we got back, parked up on the drive, crawled off the bikes, hobbled over to each other and burst out laughing. I would have said to Mike 'gi' me a high five' if I'd been able to lift my arm. We were so proud of ourselves, never mind that we had numb bottoms and could barely walk. I was particularly chuffed that I had managed it on my little 125. We looked at each other and grinned like too naughty school children who had just got away with something. I remember thinking 'We may be getting on but we can still do that young, mad and impetuous thing!' Once inside, I ran a hot bath and we both had a soak and then spent the rest of the day lounging around drinking coffee and reading the Sunday papers, basking in the glory of having done 90 miles on the bikes before breakfast. The next week I went out and bought some thermal lining gloves to wear inside my summer gloves.

Where to go

A good ride on some of UK's finest motorcycle routes wouldn't be complete without a break in a great biker friendly brew. There, a world of opportunities opens itself to the tired biker, like stretching one's legs without risking road rash, drinking fluids other than rain water and even eating something that does not naturally fly.

Best Brews along UKs Motorcycle Roads, www.twistyride.com

As the weather got colder and autumn set in there were fewer fine days to get out on the bikes. Our experience with the cold, on our marathon Dales run, had also left us trying to find routes where we knew for sure we could get a warm drink mid journey. A friend of ours said 'You ought to go to Matlock on a Sunday, it's full of bikers and the whole place must be geared up to giving them somewhere to get a drink and warm up' but we were still too self conscious about our riding to contemplate rolling into the equivalent of a bikers convention. My mum gave us a very graphic description of the place when, returning home from a juggling weekend in the Dales (my mum was a keen juggler) she had to drive through Matlock on a Sunday afternoon. 'Oh, ar' Jackie, you should 'ave seen it; the place wer packed wi' bikes; you couldn't hardly move for 'em. We had to crawl along behind a great gang of 'em and I thought to meself oh our Jackie and Mike would love this, I must remember to ring and tell her about it'. Our biking adventures where uppermost in her mind because the previous evening I had ridden up to the Youth Hostel in Hartington, where she and my niece Laura and my nephew Jamie were staying with their juggling troupe on a juggling weekend. I had decided that here was a great excuse to get out on the bike so after tea I had ridden up there and joined them for a cup of tea in the early evening sunshine. My mum was thrilled to see me as, living in Leeds with the rest of my extended family, we don't get to see each other that often but I also think she was proud to show the rest of her juggling troupe that her interest in unusual hobbies is something that runs in the family. It's quite funny really because we look very alike, physically, and often when I watch her juggling and passing clubs I take heart from the fact that, as my role model for growing old, my mum is quite interesting. In turn, I think she looks at me and is reminded of her own middle years when she too rode a motorbike, but more of that later.

So, the problem remained, where to go biking? We then landed upon the idea of visiting our friends who lived about 30 miles away, down a lovely long country road with nice bends in it. By nice bends I mean ones that sweep round in a gentle arc so that you don't have to drop your speed too much but can just lean out and cruise round them, your body and the machine swaying gently from side to side. On days when the road was clear and the surrounding fields were bathed in that wonderful late afternoon light that you only get in autumn, these rides felt almost magical. When we arrived at our friend's house we were always warmly welcomed by Les and Mandy and their four kids Hannah, Molly, Even and Wilf. We would spend about 45 minutes drinking hot tea and eating nice biscuits or a piece of home made cake and answering questions from the children about our bikes and what it was like to ride them. Their fascination and wonder was always a delight to see. After our first visit apparently a long discussion ensued between Molly and Evan about what sort of motorbikes they were going to have when they grew up. They both loved my chrome sparkling Virago but Evan was a bit worried that it might look too girly. I mean you have to worry about those things when you're only 6 years old, don't you? On our third or fourth visit Evan grilled me about what it was like to wear a helmet. 'Can you hear anything in a helmet? Is it dark inside?' I think it's wonderful that children seem to have a way of looking at the world that is always so refreshingly different. 'You can hear things but because motorbikes are so noisy it's quite important that they do keep some of the sound out and it's not dark inside because the light comes in through the front.' He looked at me, his little face screwed up in concentration as he tried to assimilate this new information. 'Do you want to try it on?' I prompted. His eyes opened wide with eager anticipation. 'Can I?' he asked excitedly. 'Course you can' I said as I picked up my helmet and helped him to pull it over his head. He stared out at me looking slightly nervous so I lifted the visor up. 'You okay in there'. He nodded then a little voice said 'Can I put the gloves on as well please?' I handed him the gloves but as he looked down to put them on the helmet wobbled and he quickly jerked his head up again. I squatted down in front of him and put the gloves on him. He began to grin. I could see his mouth because his head was so small in the helmet that the jaw protector piece was round his neck rather than his chin. He started to pretend he was revving up a motorbike, his laughter tinkling out of the helmet. 'Me, me, I want a go' said a tiny voice at the back of me. I turned round to find Wilf standing there. At 3 years old, Wilf wasn't much bigger than the helmet but he was determined to show that he was as brave as his big brother and could put his head inside this dark silver orb. I switched the helmet and gloves and then we all had to laugh as Wilf wobbled round the kitchen, waving his massive leather covered hands and laughing out loud at his own audacity. I never knew helmets could be so much fun.

Once we turned up to find Les and Mandy were away on a weekend break and Les's mum and dad were house and babysitting. The children greeted us in their usual friendly and excited way and so, once she had established that we were not a pair of scary, evil bikers, Les's mum invited us in for a cup of tea. Then she and Les's dad, Col, started to reminisce about their biking days. My parent's generation all seemed to ride bikes of one kind or another probably because the age of cheap mass produced cars was yet to come. In fact, trawling through some old family photograph albums with my mum I came across a picture of my grandparents and aunty Dora posing for a photograph in a photographers studio. Wearing their Sunday best clothes and smiling for the camera they are sitting on and in a motorbike and sidecar, which was obviously the thing to be seen to be doing in those days. Anyway, Col couldn't remember what make his first bike had been but thought that his second one had been a Triumph Road Rocket. What a great name. In his lovely thick Welsh accent he said 'We used to go all over on it, me and Liz, we loved it.' Liz took up the story, 'Yes and you know we didn't have any of this fancy gear you have today; no, we just used to wear our everyday clothes. I used to wear skirts and my little shoes because, you know, women didn't wear trousers in those days, oh no, so it was a bit cold sometimes.' I was amazed. 'You used to wear skirts on the pillion?' I asked, horrified. 'I certainly did' said Liz 'and I used to read books whilst we were travelling along' she said whilst demonstrating her 'reading and riding' pose. I was stunned. Col started to laugh and then said 'Oh yes and sometimes she would fall asleep so to wake her up I used to stand up on my foot pegs and let the wind blow up her skirt!' By this time, Mike and I were just lost for words, which is not unusual for Mike but pretty amazing for me. Though, in fairness, I had heard about this falling asleep on the pillion thing before from another friend of mine. She told me that her parents used to travel from the Midlands to the Isle of Man TT races on their old motorbike and her mum often fell asleep. To stop her falling off the bike her dad used to fasten her mum to him with a great big belt that went around both their waists. What a generation they were, talk about made of sterner stuff. Mind you, a few weeks after I heard that story Mike had asked me to ride pillion on his bike so he could see what it was like to ride with a passenger. In spite of all my fears about perching on the back of a fast moving machine that I have no control over I agreed to do it and I was surprised by how warm and sleepy I felt tucked in behind him as he rode round my practice left hand loop. I can quite see that it might be easy to nod off whilst riding pillion. Col then went on to tell us about the sidecar he'd bought and fitted to the Road Rocket. 'It was very useful but the bike never felt the same after that and when I came to sell it I decided to separate the bike and sidecar and sell them separately. The young fella that came to buy the sidecar spent a bit of time looking it over and then told me that he thought it must have been fixed to the bike all wrong. Something to do with the suspension not working properly. No wonder Liz always used to moan about it, saying it was uncomfortable.' Liz quickly jumped in. 'Uncomfortable, it was a nightmare. The night I went into labour with our Les he took me down to the hospital in it. It was rattling and bumping and when we finally got there I was only in labour for ten minutes!' And so the stories went on. We had such a laugh and when we started to get ready to leave I felt like a real softie putting on all my warm protective gear.

The other unofficial biking café we started visiting was Mike's sister, Kathryn, and her two daughters, Rose and Olivia. They live about 30 miles away, out the other end of town. We cover a circular route to get to them. Main roads on the way out and country lanes on the way back. Another nice ride with a good stop for tea and biscuits in the middle. Once whilst we were there Kathryn asked me if I wanted a pair of sandals which she had bought but which she said the kids hated her wearing (obviously her daughters are members of the fashion police as well as mine). They were modern leather sandals in excellent condition so I said I would be delighted to have them. Neither Mike nor I had brought a rucksack with us so the question then arose as to how I was going to get them home. 'Not to worry' I said 'I'll just stick them down the front of my jacket'. Which I did. The heels stuck out at the front, making it look like I had got a pair of small traffic cones hiding in my jacket. Kathryn hooted with laughter. 'You're not going to ride home like that are you?' she asked whilst wiping the tears from her eyes. 'You look like Madonna on a motorbike' she said. I was just thinking that maybe that wasn't such a bad thing when Mike piped up 'Yes, the Madonna with the big boobies'. I looked at him, whilst Kathryn rolled around laughing in the background, and he grinned, a cheeky, eyebrows raised grin and said 'Well, I think you look very nice'. So that day I rode home looking about 20 years younger, well at least I thought I looked 20 year younger and when we got back I felt a little twinge of regret when I had to remove my temporary implants and deflate back to my normal self. Mike looked a bit disappointed too.

Practice makes perfect

Try not. Do or do not, there is no try.
Yoda, Jedi Master, Star Wars

One evening, having just put down the phone after hearing
from my daughter that her boyfriend had failed his driving test
for the second time, I turned to Mike and said 'James ought to
forget about cars and learn to ride a motorbike, it would be much
cheaper. He loves bikes and he would only have to pay for his
CBT and then he could ride round on L plates for a few years
until he could afford a car'. Mike looked up from stacking the
dishwasher, it was his turn as I had cooked tea, and said 'Well
you're wrong on a few counts there.' 'What do you mean?' I
asked as I headed off to the living room with my cup of coffee.
I never watch him tidy up the kitchen because I hate it when he
does it to me. I waited for the machine to woosh into action and
Mike to join me in the living room. 'Well, for a start it won't be

cheap because the insurance for young riders is astronomical and secondly he can't ride round for a few years on L plates because the CBT is only valid for two years and then you have to take it again.' I had forgotten about that, though, now I came to think about it I did remember Lee saying something like that to me when he handed over my CBT certificate. So, maybe getting a motorbike was not the answer for James but then I began to think about my situation. 'So I'll need to redo my CBT when two years is up, won't I, unless ...' I looked at Mike and waited for him to finish my sentence. He just looked back at me and said nothing. He always has been reluctant to play verbal games. 'So, if I don't want to redo my CBT, what have I got to do? Remind me.' As he scanned down the TV listings page in the paper looking for something, anything, decent to watch, he said 'You know what you have to do. You've got to pass a road test for motorbikes.' It was coming back to me now. That's right, I needed to take my test and then I could ride without L plates for two years and then I could get a bigger bike if I wanted. 'Perhaps I should try and do my test on the Virago and then I wouldn't need to retake my CBT' I said, half to myself, as I mulled it over. 'What's the point of that? If you're going to take your test you might as well take it on a bigger bike and then you've got the choice. You can either carry on riding the 125, which I can't believe for one minute you'll want to do once you've ridden a bigger bike, or you can get a bigger bike straight away' he said, wearing his 'What are you like?' expression on his face. I could feel my hackles starting to rise. 'I don't need a bigger bike, I love my bike and it is quite powerful enough for me' I said, adopting an 'Oh you men and your bigger bikes' attitude. 'Well, it's up to you, but in any case you need to do your theory test first because you can't do any test until you've passed that' he said in a tone of voice which suggested that that was the end of that little conversation. But I wasn't that easily deterred. 'So the theory test, did you do that?' I asked, speaking over the television, which was now on and showing a programme about sharks. Mike watches all the programmes about sharks, which I always find a bit odd but, I suppose, a man has to have his interests. It's a bit like men and sheds. Lots of men have them and love them and I can't for the life of me see why, I mean they're just huts in the garden aren't they? Mike has never gone for sheds but he has his own office which is full of bits and pieces from his days as an art student, his many and varied interests over the years, not to mention all his work stuff, so maybe that's the equivalent of his shed. Anyway, with one eye on a great white lurking in the murky depths he said 'You know I did it'. I could see this was going to be another one of those pulling teeth conversations. 'So what do you have to do in a theory test?' I could tell that my persistent questioning was beginning to irritate him but I wanted to know. Then he said something really useful. 'Look, upstairs is a CD which you can practice on, it has the sort of questions you will be asked about the highway code and stuff. It's on my bottom shelf in the office. If you want to know what to do, go and get that and have a go with it' and he turned back to his programme. I jumped up and shot upstairs to his office, determined to track down this CD and see what this theory test was all about. I eventually found it, buried in a pile of technical CDs full of computer software for our business machines. This was the 'work pile' of CDs as opposed to the 'pleasure pile' of music CDs. Mike loves listening to music whilst he works and has a big collection of all kinds of stuff so I felt pretty pleased with myself that I had tracked down the one CD I needed so quickly. So how to use it? I took it through to my computer and switched it on and waited for it to boot up. Using computers for me is a bit like riding motorbikes, they are great things to use but I have no real idea how they work. Whenever my machine plays up or I need something installed I usually yell 'MMMIIIKKKE' and drag him away from whatever he is doing to sort it out. Recently, however, he has been encouraging me to sort things out more myself because he and I know that my damsel in distress mode is just a cover for laziness on my part. So I decided to try and install it myself. About half an hour later, with me grinding my teeth in frustration, Mike came into the room and said 'How're you getting on with it?' then looked at the screen and saw that I was up to my eyeballs in error messages. 'What are you doing?' he asked, looking perplexed and coming round the desk to get a better look at my sorry effort. 'I don't know, it just won't work, it keeps coming up with this error message thing, I hate computers ..' I whined pathetically. 'Oh move over, let me sort it out' he said as I vacated my chair and handed it all over to him. I stood behind him grinning. It was wonderful having such willing computer support on hand like this. Mike used to spend half his life on the phone having conversations with family members that started with things like 'Mike, can you just talk me through this? I've put my CD in the drawer and …' and 'Mike, I can't get this printer to work, do you think I should ..' and so on. After a while he became a bit weary of running a one man IT help desk and when the phone rang he would shake his head and mouth at me 'I'm not in if it's anything to do with computers'. Fortunately we now have other IT experts coming up through the ranks. My stepson Graeme is a real whizz at it and often helps Mike out now and James, the failed driver, is also very good too and so he now handles the Leeds end of things. Incidentally James passed his driving test third time and is now happily zooming around in his little Peugeot, though having seen my 'hog', as he calls it, I know he is secretly lusting after a motorbike of his own. So Mike got the Theory test CD installed and I started to work through the questions. It was a revelation. Having been a car driver for over 25 years I realized, and I hate to admit this, that I didn't really know what half the signs on the road meant, I only vaguely understood what road markings were all about and I had no idea at all about the rules that applied to motorbikes. How embarrassing. I spent a week slaving over the CD every night and then Mike prompted me to ring up and book a theory test to 'give you a deadline to aim for'. My test date came through for a month later. I had just a month to become a knowledgeable road user.

Over the next few weeks I drove Mike mad every time we went out in the car. 'What does that sign mean?' and 'So those longer white lines in the middle of the road say it is getting more dangerous and to take more care, don't they?' Mike was amazed and a little worried that I didn't know all this, especially as a large part of my role in our business involved driving all around the country running training courses. 'Surely you know that?' he would reply to some of my questions. 'Yes, of course, but I'm just checking' I would say hoping he didn't look at my face and see that that was not the case. I realised that I did sort of know the rules of the road and I am a safe driver, I've never had an accident or a speeding ticket or anything, but after 25 years it was more like having a general awareness than a specific knowledge. Also a lot of road signs make sense in context but just looking at them in a book or on the computer screen is much harder. Anyway I practiced and practiced. When I wasn't doing practice tests in the evening I was reading the Highway Code in bed. 'For goodness sake' Mike said, one night as I tried to pick his brains about whether motorbikes could tow trailers on the motorway. 'It's only a theory test, not an A level in the Highway Code. Don't you think you're overdoing it a bit?' I tried to ignore him. I have always been hopeless at exams and tests. Even when I really know my stuff I can still go to pieces under exam conditions. 'Look, shut up, I don't know this stuff and my test is next week' I wailed, my plan to ignore him scuppered by my inability to say nothing when asked a question. The strong, silent approach is impossible for chatterboxes like me. 'You do know it. You've been learning this stuff for weeks now, in fact, if you don't know it by now you shouldn't be driving round on the roads' he said climbing into bed. He started to read some novel or other and I looked at him enviously. I too had a big pile of novels at the side of the bed. I love reading and get through about a novel a week. You can't beat sitting in bed with a cup of tea, getting lost in the Bayou Teche in a James Lee Burke novel or spending the morning on some smallholding watching ex pats make a fool of themselves as they try to establish the good life in some Spanish village or other. But all that had to be put aside whilst I slogged my way through the Highway Code for the umpteenth time.

The day of the test arrived and I was a nervous wreck. Mike asked me if I was going to go up to the test centre on my bike as it was 20 miles away in the neighbouring town. 'No I am not biking up there, I've got enough to worry about without biking there' I said as I did some last minute revision. I drove up and quickly found a parking space and, in fact, arrived about ten minutes early. A tall, elderly gentleman came out of a little room and I gave him my appointment letter. He invited me to follow him into the room so that he could get a few details from me. 'Now then, you've come to do your theory test .. oh your motorbike theory test' he said sounding a bit surprised. 'So you want to ride a motorbike' he

said using a tone of voice that seemed to imply 'Really, someone your age ought to know better'. He then explained to me how the test was done and where I would need to sit and what I would have to do. Just as I thought the conversation was about to end, a slightly younger man, sitting across the room at another desk, piped up 'Have you got one of those Harley Davidsons then?' I smiled weakly and replied 'No, but I'd like one'. The older gentleman began to shake his head and said 'I've never been one for motorbikes myself' and I was just about to say 'Well that doesn't matter does it because it's not you that wants to ride one, is it?' when he gave me a lovely smile and said 'Well, good luck dear' and I decided to just go and do the test. The test was really easy. I couldn't believe it. It was just like all the practice ones I had done and I rattled through it. When I had finished I went back out into the waiting area and hung around to get my results. The elderly gentleman came out of his office with my certificate and a letter and a great big smile on his face. There were other people waiting by now so he handed me the certificate and then began to point at the letter, doing a sort of nod and a wink action at me. What on earth was he doing? I looked at him and then down at the letter. He was pointing to a line which stated CONGRATULATIONS! You answered all items correctly.
I was flabbergasted. I'd got full marks in a test. I thanked him and rushed outside to ring Mike. 'Guess what?' I yelled excitedly into the phone. 'You passed' he said, matter of factly. 'Yes, I passed and with full marks, not one wrong answer, good eh?' By this time I was jumping up and down on the spot with unsuppressed glee. 'Well I should hope so, the amount of revision you've done, I wouldn't expect anything else – by the way, on your way home can you get some milk, we've run out' he said. Talk about being brought down to earth. 'Oh okay, see you in a bit' I said and set

off to the supermarket. Any cars passing me on the way home must have thought I was on drugs or something because I just couldn't stop giggling.

Time to go large

They always say time changes things, but you actually have to change them yourself.
Andy Warhol

Then winter set in and once again the bikes were put into hibernation, oiled, snug under their covers and, thanks to the house move, settled into the garage. As the days shortened and the long, dark evenings set in I found I really missed being out on the bikes. In my mind, our summer rides became a series of nostalgic memories of us two playmates, riding around the place, visiting friends and family and enjoying the countryside and our bikes. How wonderful. What more could anyone ask for? Well in my case, possibly a slightly bigger bike. Now I really thought about it I had to admit that, yes, I had had a wonderful time but no, I didn't like being left behind on the hills all the time. It was hard watching Mike sail off into the distance whilst I dropped down through the gears and accelerated like mad to keep up with him. The other thing I didn't like was that, at times like that, the bike sounded more like a sewing machine on steroids than a cool cruiser. I began to toy with the idea of getting a bigger bike. 'Mike, do you think I should get a bigger bike?' I asked him one evening as we relaxed after a hard day in the office. 'What do you mean?' he said, barely looking up from his newspaper. What did I mean? Was he deaf or just suffering from a temporary drop in I.Q., which I've noticed can happen when he's asked about things he doesn't want to discuss. For example, 'Mike, what are you doing with that big pile of old newspapers in the living room? 'What do you mean, what am I doing with that big pile of old newspapers?' he'll reply. I'll then say, speaking very slow and clearly, 'I said - what are you doing with that big pile of old newspapers?' To which he'll reply 'I'm not doing anything with that big pile of old newspapers.' Then I'll say 'I know that ..' and so on. See what I mean? So immediately I began to wonder why he might not want to discuss this topic. I decided to press on. 'Do you think I should get a bigger bike, you know, a bigger motorbike?' He looked up, an alert look on his face like he'd just heard a strange noise upstairs. 'A bigger bike? What - instead of the 125? I thought you loved that bike.' I thought about this for a minute. He was right, I did love that bike but I wanted it to go up hills more easily. 'I do love it but do you remember when we met that biker at the reservoir and he said his mate had a 535 version of the Virago which he loved? Well, maybe I could get a bigger version of this bike and then I could get up the hills' I said, trying to make it sound like a minor adjustment we were discussing here. Mike wasn't fooled. 'Well, you've changed your tune' he said, yet again. I groaned, 'Oh don't start that again, it's not like I want some great monster of a bike, just one that will go

up hills'. He wasn't going to let me get off that easily. 'You've always said' and at this point he started speaking in a squeaky high pitched voice, 'a 125 is powerful enough for me, I don't need anything bigger than that'. I could feel my teeth starting to clench and my eyes narrowing to slits. Why did he do that? I never talk like that. Okay, I might whine a bit now and again and sometimes I have been known to use my 'Oh go on dad, let me voice' when I want to wheedle something out of him but a dumb blonde, Marilyn Monroe, Some Like It Hot voice? Never. Sensing that the bull might be lining up to charge he quickly decided to change tack. 'Look, if you want a bigger bike you've got to do your Direct Access Course' he said. 'Oh' I groaned, remembering how exhausted he had looked after some of his lessons and just as I was beginning to go right off the idea I noticed that he was looking at me and smiling. 'What?' I said. He kept looking at me, obviously processing this new possibility in his mind, and then said 'Yes, that's a great idea actually, you ought to do your Direct Access Course and then get a bigger bike and then we could really start to go places. I mean, that 125 is hopeless for long journeys but if you had a bigger one we could go all over the place.'
I started to feel nervous. 'What do you mean, go all over the place?' I asked, wondering if my I.Q. levels had suddenly dropped too. Mike began to look wistful. 'Well, don't you ever wish that you could do something awesome in your own life, something that pushed you to the limit, something that you could look back on later and say I did that and it would be amazing?' I was totally confused, what had this got to do with me doing the Direct Access Course? I knew he'd found it a challenge but surely it wasn't that bad? 'What do you mean 'something awesome'?' I asked. 'Well like motorbiking across America or something' he replied, staring into space dreamily. I was stunned. Where did this come

from? 'You want me to get a bigger bike so we can motorbike across America' I spluttered. Over the years I've told myself that I've learnt to read Mike like a book but then every so often he says or does something that makes me think there are whole chunks of him that are still a complete mystery to me, and to him I suspect. So where did this come from? As I pressed him for an explanation, in fact, for a detailed break down of all the thought processes that lay behind this incredible statement, he became more elusive. 'No, it was just a thought' he said, turning back to his paper. Just as I was about to move into top gear in the husband and wife interrogation stakes, I stopped myself and looked at him. Why was I so obsessed with getting an explanation? It was just a thought that had popped into his head, a wonderful, dreamy, escapist kind of a thought and here was I ruining it by trying to disassemble it. Why did I have to always be so logical and practical? Why couldn't I be a dreamer too. I watched him reading his paper and realised that, in fact, I was very lucky to be married to a man who, approaching the age of 50, still thought of his life as being full of possibilities, still wanted adventures and still saw life as being out there waiting to be lived. 'Really, do you think we could do something like that?' I asked him, tentatively. 'No, it was a daft idea, just forget it' he said dismissively. For a minute I was almost disappointed before checking myself. Mike and I often do this to each other. One comes up with an idea that the other thinks is ridiculous, but then is slowly won round just as the other goes off the original idea. I call it the swings and roundabout effect. He will swing at something and I will swing away but then come back to it in a roundabout fashion, and visa versa. I could see that this conversation might go that way if I was not careful, so I dropped it. A few weeks later I came across Tom Cunliffe's book, Good Vibrations – Coast to coast by Harley, in which he writes about how he and his wife Roz rode across America on two Harley Davidsons. I bought it and showed it to Mike. 'Look at this, this couple did what you were on about, you know, motorbiking across America.' He read the notes on the back cover and looked at me, grinning with a 'told you it could be done' look on his face. I read the book and it did, in fact, confirm for me what I had suspected all along, namely that you would have to be completely bonkers to take on such an endurance test of a journey. Interestingly, at the end Tom says that Roz, since returning to England hasn't 'taken on another bike and she still won't travel on the back of mine' so perhaps it put her off for life, and from reading the book I can see why! Mike, having read the book, disagreed and said it sounded like a fantastic experience. Maybe I'm just not cut out for epic adventures.

During those winter months we started buying biking magazines to try and learn a bit more about bikes, to overcome the problem of looking like complete cluts's when talking to other bikers. A lot of these magazines are actually very well written and many of the articles are very funny to read. Particularly entertaining are the short descriptions they give to different bikes in the bike review sections. One day I caught Mike having a good laugh whilst reading through one lot of listings. When I asked him what was so funny he said 'You should see what they've written here about the Yamaha Virago 535, you know the one you like. They describe it as 'A Tarts' Handbag' he said, grinning. 'Don't be daft, let me look' I said as I pulled the magazine off him. And there it was, A Tart's Handbag. I read the rest of the description and it was clear that, at least in that magazine, the Virago was seen as a girly bike or a bike for people who wanted a flashy looking little cruiser with a very low seat. I was miffed. Then as I read the descriptions of the other bikes I realised that almost all makes were fair game. Some big tourers were described as Gin Palaces on Wheels and Motorbikes as House; some speed bikes were written up as 'all-singing, all-dancing, all-costing' and 'think of your favourite aunty, friendly, helpful and does the job'; a trial bike described as 'as mad as a fish on a rollerskate' and so on. Very soon, I too was giggling with delight as some of these amusing little potted descriptions, but a tart's handbag for goodness sake. I decided to go looking for a magazine that specialised in cruisers but they did not seem to be as readily available as the magazines that were for fans of sports bikes. Then one day in W H Smiths I spotted a magazine with a cruiser on the front but unfortunately it was heat sealed inside a plastic cover so I couldn't get a look at the contents. I bought it anyway and took it home to read. When I opened it up it was full of customised easy rider type motorbikes mainly being used as props for practically naked women to loll all over. Captions like Cindy loves the feel of this hot rod between her legs and Suzie knows she will get the ride of her life on this one! were everywhere. I was embarrassed. Did anyone I know see me buying it? I showed it to Mike in disgust and he spent ages checking it out. 'You don't need to read it from cover to cover' I snapped. 'I'm not reading, I'm looking' he said. I threw it away much to his chagrin. 'There were some really interesting bikes in there' he said. Yeh, right.

Later that week Mike brought a wonderful book home from the library. It was called 'Berry on Bikes, the Top 100' and it was full of hilarious descriptions of Steve Berry's selection of the top 100 bikes of all time – he used to be a presenter on Top Gear. I was delighted because the Virago 535 was in there. Okay, it was described as the 'Best bike for petite girls in leather mini skirts', which was a bit worrying as I am not petite and certainly haven't got the legs for mini skirts, but it went on to say that the Virago was probably one of the best mid sized cruisers ever made and was ideal for riders starting a career on two-wheels. I felt vindicated. 'Read that' I said to Mike 'you see, I was right, the Virago is an ideal bike for someone like me'. He read through the piece, a smile playing across his lips. 'You're right, yes, it's a girly bike' he said. What is it with these men? They love bikes with names like Monster, Bandit, Fireblade, Marauder, Hornet, Raptor, Thundercat. I could just imagine the manufacturers sitting around saying things like 'Can anyone come up with a name that means speed, power, danger, masculinity and testosterone?' Only Harley Davidson, as far as I can see, buck this trend and come up with names for their bikes that, in most other situations, would get them a punch in the mouth. 'Sir, you look like the sort of man that should be riding a Fat Boy or a Wide Glide.' I am sure that the names of bikes have a big effect on how they are seen by bikers. When I looked up the word Virago in the dictionary I found that it had two meanings. Virago: bad tempered or abusive woman or female warrior. So, a sort of Boadicea machine for pre-menstrual women, maybe that was how it came to be seen as a girly bike! Perhaps, if the manufacturers wanted to attract more women into biking, they could come up with less threatening names for the bikes. I mused on this for a while. Mike asked me what I was thinking about. 'More girly names for bikes' I said. Mike looked at me with one of his 'Oh no, here she goes again' looks on his face. 'Well for example, you could have a Kawasaki Kitten or a Honda Freedom or a Suzuki Dreamer, you know, something like that' I said wistfully. Mike shook his head and said 'Well Honda used to do a Super Dream but if you look at Berry's book he says it was neither super nor a dream so maybe that's not such a good idea, besides blokes wouldn't buy them with names like that'. I rest my case.

Snubbed for being a biker

For most travelers the journey is a means to an end. When you go by bike, the travel is an end in itself. You ride through places you've never been, experience it all, meet new people, have an adventure. Things don't get much better than this.
Investment Biker: Around the world with Jim Rogers

Winter over, the weather started to improve and we got back on the bikes. It was wonderful to be out in the fresh air again, feeling the wind on our faces and the sunshine warm on our backs. Even though you are completely wrapped up in the C-3PO biking gear, motorbiking still makes you feel like you are out there in the elements, which is great when the sun is shining and it's warm and balmy but not so good when it's raining and cold. I have nothing but admiration for those bikers who commute to work every day in all kinds of weather. I have only been caught in the rain a handful of times, but every time I have quickly headed home, struggling to see clearly through my wet visor and desperately trying to monitor the road surface for slippery spots like manhole covers and painted road markings. Not much fun. But sunny days are a dream. So off we went again, zipping around to visit people and places and generally enjoying that feeling of freedom and daring-do that biking gives you. Then Mike strained his back digging out a huge trench to lay a cold water mains pipe at the side of the new house. 'Will you hurry up and get better 'cos we're missing good biking weather' I moaned at him one weekend, as he tottered around the house looking like Mrs Overall from Acorn Antiques. 'Look, I can't help it if my back's done in, you go on your own if you're that desperate' he said, grimacing with pain. For a moment I thought that perhaps it wasn't very nice to leave him to struggle on his own but that moment passed and I went and got my bike gear on. So off I went on my travels. Sometimes I just rode around the surrounding villages and countryside before calling in on my friend Kath for a quick cup of tea and a chat. Other times I went up to the industrial estate, near the bike school, to practice slow riding and U turns. One of the roads on the estate puts out traffic cones at the weekend, something to do with fire hazards, and I used to ride around those in figures of eights and do U turns. Why did I do this? Well by now I had decided that I did want to try and get the big sister version of my bike, the Virago 535, never mind what Mike or all the other blokes thought, and so had booked onto a Direct Access Course. I had decided to do it all in one week, in mid summer when our business is traditionally very quiet. Having made the decision I set about practicing all the things Mike had said would be tested like U turns, hill starts, slow riding and town riding. When I explained to Mike what I was doing he groaned. 'Oh no, not the theory test all over again' he said. The theory test, what was he on about, I had done that. 'What do you mean?'

I asked, puzzled. 'Well, let me guess, by the time you come to
do the course you'll have practiced everything a million times,
discussed and analysed everything so much that on the day you'll
be able to do the test blindfolded and you'll drive me and yourself
mad in the process. How long is it before you do this course?'
he asked, looking weary. 'It's about two months away' I replied
indignantly, thinking that there's nothing wrong with a bit of
practice and my riding is still not that good anyway and well, it
pays to prepare for these things. Mike just groaned as he struggled
to get up off the couch and go put the kettle on.

Early one evening, after completing another session on the
industrial estate, I decided to pop in on a friend whose husband
had been a keen biker for years until one day, whilst driving his
car, he was involved in a horrific accident that resulted in him
losing a leg. Once back at home, after a long period of intensive
care, then physiotherapy, rest and rehabilitation, he decided he
would have to sell his beloved sports bike because he was no
longer able to get on and off it or put it onto it's centre stand.
His wife Anne said to me 'I've told our Norman all about you
and your biking and he says he'd love to see your bike, bring it
round some time will ya', so I decided to call in on my way home.
Norman came out to take a look, limping heavily on his newly
fitted artificial leg. He looked at the bike and said 'That's a nice
little bike you've got there, you've kept that nice' so I waxed
lyrical about my little dream machine. Then Norman asked me if
he could sit on it. I said 'I don't know Norman, can you sit on it?'
He looked carefully at it and then asked me to hold the handlebars
whilst he swung his good leg over the very low seat. There he sat,
the biggest grin on his face. 'Do you know, I think I could manage
one of these, it's so low you see, I can get my leg over and I can

flick the side stand down with my hand whilst I'm sitting here. Mind you, it would have to be adapted to an automatic with the gears on the handlebars but I bet it could be done'. He looked so excited it brought a lump to my throat. I turned to Anne who was standing nearby looking quite nervous. 'Anne, he's going to want one now, don't blame me, you asked me to bring it round' I said knowing I would be in for some stick later if he did get it into his head that he wanted one and Anne was against it. However, Anne just smiled. I think she was pleased to see Norman so happy and if he wanted an adapted bike, well they'd face that hurdle when they got to it. As I drove off I wandered what I'd started with that one short visit. A few weeks later I watched a man with a terrible wasting disease being interviewed on the local news, about a medical breakthrough that might lead to a cure for his illness. As he struggled to get his breathe he said 'If I could just get enough breath to have one more go on my motorbike I would be a happy man'. Now that did make me cry because I think I partly understood what he was talking about. This motorbike thing gets under your skin and the thought of never being able to ride again, once you have experienced the sheer feeling of joy and freedom that it gives you, is not something that you want to contemplate.

Another weekend, following a row with Mike over something or other, I can't remember what, I decided to go a bit further afield. I find that when I am feeling fed up or stressed if I go out for a ride I soon relax and cheer up. It's something to do with living in the moment and forgetting about everything else. One man wrote about a similar feeling in a letter to one of the biking magazines. He said that when the wife and kids were driving him mad, the minute he put on his helmet the world seemed okay. He was wondering whether he should, in fact, wear his helmet

all the time! Anyway, I love gardening and am a member of the
Royal Horticultural Society, having joined several years ago.
My membership entitles me to free entry to a number of gardens
and places of horticultural interest. So I got out my Members
Handbook to check out gardens within biking distance. I wanted
to visit one garden I had visited a couple of years ago but when
I looked at the map of how to get there I discovered that the
route was quite complicated. I began to wonder about how you
map read when you're biking. Our road atlas is massive, one of
these great big easy to read, three miles to an inch things which
is about the size of a tabloid newspaper but thicker. There was
no way I could take that with me. So I decided to write all the
road numbers down on a piece of paper to go in my pocket but
then realised that I would have to keep stopping to read it and
that would drive me mad and ruin the journey. I thought about
writing the road numbers on my hand but my gloves would cover
that so that was no use either. In the end I decided to head for
an arboretum in Cheshire that could be reached by sticking to
one road, from a town that I knew how to get to without a map.
I packed my camera, purse, mobile phone, some water, a bar of
chocolate and my Breakdown Assist Card into my rucksack and
set off. It was a lovely day and the riding was an absolute joy with
light traffic, open roads and glorious sunshine. However, the very
last part of the journey took me into unmarked country lanes and
I soon found that I had lost my way. I headed for the centre of a
village close to where I thought the arboretum must be. I ended
up parked outside a beautiful, picturesque pub, with tables, chairs
and parasols in the front of a cottage style building covered in
window boxes overflowing with the most beautiful displays of
flowers. I parked up next to the two very expensive looking cars
outside, so that I could go in and ask for directions. I went into the

pub, tugging off my helmet, and approached the bar. The barman came over and said, in a very polite voice 'Hello, can I help you at all?', with an expression on his face which seemed to say 'let me help you to leave this pub as quickly as possible'. I smiled, equally politely and said 'I am looking for an arboretum that is supposed to be somewhere near here – do you know where it is, please?' He looked at me with a confused expression on his face. 'An arber – what, sorry? Is it a farm or something?' he said, again in a polite voice. 'No, it's an arboretum, which is a collection of beautiful trees' I said, thinking that this was obviously going to be a waste of time. Then suddenly his face lit up 'Oh the arboretum' he said 'Yes, it's just round here behind us' and he led me out of the pub and around to a small gate at the side. I gave him a lovely smile and he said 'Would you like me to look after your helmet for you whilst you have a wander round, I can keep it behind the bar for you if you like'. I smiled again and said thank you that would be lovely and handed it over with my gloves before venturing through the gate. What a nice man. It's funny really but when people see your bike and gear they seem to jump to all sorts of conclusions about what sort of person you are, namely some sort of dangerous rebel type who is bound to cause trouble. In my experience, however, most bikers are lovely both on and off their bikes. Some can go a bit Jack Nicholson when they get on their bikes, especially if they are super fast racing speed bikes, but nearly all are really nice people when you take the time to just chat to them, though they might not like me for saying that. In some ways it is quite nice being thought of as a rebel and I know I love it when people say 'You ride a motorbike?' with awe and wonder in their voice. It is nice to have that effect but it is not nice when it is taken a step further and people avoid or shun you out of some sort of fear of bikers.

Anyway, I spent a good hour exploring and photographing the arboretum and then headed back to the pub. At the bar the man was nowhere to be seen so I asked a young barmaid if I could have my helmet back and oh, did they serve coffee please? She looked down her nose at me and said 'We do, but it costs £1.95' as if that would put an end to that request. Conclusion jumped to, number two. Bikers are only interested in mugs of tea at 60p a throw. I said that would be fine and would it be too much trouble to ask if it could be served out on the terrace? Served out on the terrace, well I thought, a bit of Sloane Ranger wouldn't go amiss here. She was suitably impressed and my cafetiere of coffee, silver cream jug and after coffee biscuit were duly served up. I chuckled to myself as I savoured what was actually a very good cup of coffee and then struggled back into my gear and headed home.

From mama to nana

If I had known how wonderful it would be to have grandchildren,
I'd have had them first.
Lois Wyse

A few weeks later, whilst visiting my family in Leeds, I received
some momentus news. It all came about in a strange way. There
I was, helping my mum to chop down a dying conifer in her
garden, when the phone rang. 'It's ar' Kathryn fur you' shouted
my dad who was watching the proceedings from his wheelchair.
As I walked back to the house I could hear him talking to Kathryn
on the phone. 'There at it again, Wyn and yer mam, cutting down
a tree …. Well you know what ther' like .. always up to sommat ..'
I took the phone from him feeling slightly anxious. Kathryn was
away studying in Berlin and didn't usually call during the day
because of the cost. 'Hello love, what's up?' I asked in a false,
breezy manner because I know that both my girls get exasperated

with the way I always fear the worst when they call unexpectedly. 'Oh nothing's the matter, I just wanted to see how you were and have a chat' she said. Bit strange, I thought, but then I relaxed and sat down and had a chat with her. Towards the end of the conversation she asked me for her sister's phone number saying she didn't have it with her in Germany. 'Why the rush to ring Helen, you're coming back in two weeks you could ring her then' I said as I went to track down the number. 'Oh, it's just that I haven't spoken to her in ages and thought I would give her a ring' said Kathryn. Always keen to promote sibling harmony I gave her the number and said 'I'm seeing Helen later today, do you want me to get her to ring you?'. 'No, that's okay, I'll ring her' she said and we said our goodbyes and I got back to my lumberjacking.

Later that day I went round to my younger daughter's flat and was busy telling her all about chopping down the conifer when she looked at me, a worried expression on her face, and said 'Mum, I've got something to tell you'. My worry alarm started ringing loudly in my head. 'What?' I asked, a terrible sinking feeling in my stomach. 'I'm pregnant' she said. I looked at her face and suddenly I could see her as she was when she was a little girl and we had been staying at her other grandmas. For some reason that I cannot remember, there was a fruit bowl with money in it, in one of the rooms and a five pound note had gone missing. As none of the adults wanted or needed the money, suspicion fell on the girls. I took them into the bedroom, sat them down and explained what was missing and then said that it was very important not to take other people's things because you might get their things now but you would lose their trust later and it wasn't nice to not be trusted by people. They sat listening to me, their beautiful little faces knotted in concentration, and then Helen's face took on the

same expression that she was wearing now, the look that said
Oops, I've done something naughty, mummy's going to be cross.
She immediately went and got the money from under her pillow
and explained that she was just saving it for grandma and then, as
now, I was not cross but relieved to know the truth. So I asked her
how she felt about the baby and she said a bit shocked but happy.
Apparently she had been worrying about telling me because
she had feared that I would be disappointed in her and that this
would show in my face and she could not bear that. However,
she was feeling slightly less worried because, and this was the
strange thing, Kathryn had rung her that morning and said 'Helen,
are you pregnant?' Helen admitted that she was and asked how
Kathryn knew. Kathryn explained that she had been sat eating her
breakfast and suddenly a powerful image of Helen and a baby
had come into her mind and she just knew Helen was pregnant.
Kathryn was thrilled and delighted and told Helen she couldn't
wait to be an aunty, so Helen was feeling a bit more confident
about telling me. When I heard this part of the tale I started to
worry that I now had one daughter who was pregnant and one
who was a witch!

So, I was going to be a grandma. I sat there thinking I was too
young to be a grandma and Helen was certainly too young to
be a mum but in spite of all of that I couldn't help feeling a bit
thrilled myself. How wonderful, a new baby in the family, and
with her steady job, the support of her boyfriend James and the
love of her family all around her I just knew she was going to
make a smashing mum. I jumped up and hugged her. 'Oh Helen,
you always did want to do everything early. Congratulations, I'm
sure everything will work out fine, now come on, let's go tell your
nana. I can't wait to tell her she's going to be a great grandma!'

When we got round to my mum's I told her I had some news. 'What?' she said, as she bustled past me with the washing. 'Well the first bit of news is that I'm going to be a very young grandma'. She looked at me, a bit confused, so before there was time for that to really sink in I went on to say 'and if you think that's bad well what's even worse is that you are going to be a great grandma!' I couldn't help it but I started laughing because my mum is so young at heart that for her to be a great grandma just seemed so ridiculous. Helen stood there looking a little sheepish whilst my mum struggled to make sense of this news. 'What..? Who..?' she stuttered and then her face filled with a huge grin. 'Helen, it's you isn't it … well, love, how lovely, you're taking after your nana' and before there was time for her to explain she grabbed Helen and started hugging her. Helen grinned and then, taking a step back, she said 'What do you mean nana – I'm taking after you?' My mum took hold of Helen's hand and said 'Well I met your granddad when I was 15, same as you and James. I married him when I was 16, but you young uns don't do that nowadays so ignore that bit, and I had your mum when I was 19, same as you'll be – so there you are, you're taking after me' and as she said this she looked over at me with an expression on her face which said 'see, everything's going to be fine'. I, however, couldn't resist picking up my earlier theme, 'Yes, but mum you're going to be a GREAT grandma' I said, mischievously. 'I'm already great, and a grandma' she replied, quick as a flash so I decided I needed to up the stakes a bit. 'Yes but I'll be a glamorous granny on a motorbike'. 'Huh - I'll be more glamorous than you…' she taunted, but before we could say anymore Helen butted in and said 'Stop it, the pair of you, it's not a competition'. I agreed but my mum, with a twinkle in her eye said 'It could be' and we all fell about laughing again.

Later that day I rang Mike to tell him the news. He was a bit shocked and didn't seem to know what to say, so I said we could talk about it when I got back the following day. The rest of the weekend was spent drawing up battle plans to get Helen and James out of their rented flat and into a little house of their own in time for the new arrival. I promised them I would return the following weekend to go house hunting.

Back home I asked Mike what he thought about becoming a granddad. 'But I'm not going to be a granddad' he said, obviously thinking that the offspring of stepchildren don't make you eligible for grandparent status. 'Well, technically, I suppose you will be a step granddad which isn't quite so bad' I said, mulling it over. 'No, what's bad is that I'm now going to be sleeping with a grandma' he said, a cheeky look on his face. 'What do you mean?' I spluttered 'you'll be a granddad too'. He shook his head, 'No, you're the granny in this house and I'm still a young man'. I looked at his face, he was loving this, the rat. Then the phone rang. It was Kathryn, eager to discuss the news. We chatted for a while and then she said 'How does Mike feel about becoming a granddad?' I explained that he did not see himself as a granddad, to which she laughed and said 'Well he might like to think that but whilst ever he's living with you he is going to be a granddad – Granddad Mike.' I relayed all this to Mike, with a 'told you so' expression on my face, and pointed out that whilst he might not want to think of himself as a granddad, everyone else in the family would. He looked at me thoughtfully and then, with a mischievous look in his eye he said 'Well, if I'm going to be a granddad I want a V Rod'.

'A V Rod? A Harley Davidson V Rod?' I gasped. 'Yes, a V

Rod' he replied dreamily. I couldn't believe my ears. The Harley Davidson V Rod was the new golden wonder of the motorcycle world. A brand new Harley after 100 years of motorbike production and the best ever made, according to all the biking magazines. Developed from technologies refined in the American VR 1000 Superbike race programme and designed in conjunction with Porsche, the V Rod is a superb, beautifully designed, awesome to ride and mega, mega expensive motorbike. I stood there, dumbstruck for at least ten seconds, which is a long time for me. 'You are kidding, you don't like Harleys' I said, knowing full well that this did not extend to the V Rod. We had been reading reviews on it all winter and marvelling at its beauty and styling. Not one critic seemed to have a bad word to say about it, even sports bikers were taking an interest. Mike looked at me, reflected for a moment and then said 'No, I'm not keen on Harleys but the V Rod is in a class of it's own'. Just in time I realised that we were now walking in that border country between 'it's only an idea' and 'I'm definitely going to do this' so I pulled back to rethink my tactics. 'Well, it's an interesting idea, perhaps, we should have a look at one' I said carefully, hoping that this little show of support might have the opposite effect and make Mike pull back from the idea. 'Yes, I think I might book a test ride on one' he said as he turned to leave the room. Damn. Then I thought to myself 'No, it's a cruiser, he doesn't like cruisers, he's only doing this to wind me up' and I decided to put it out of mind as I had lots of other things to do, like contact all my mates and let them know I was about to become a granny on a motorbike!

100 miles on a 125cc

---

*I don't know what it is, but there's something special about
a long distance motorcycle trip. Maybe it's the excitement of
getting to spend a good chunk of time exploring somewhere new.
Or, maybe it's the prospect of getting to spend a lot of time on a
motorcycle. Whatever it is ... one thing I definitely know is that I
get just as excited now, as I did the first time.*
Tips for a long distance motorcycle trip,
www.openroadjourney.com

A couple of days later I reminded Mike of my plans to go back
up to Leeds to help Helen house hunt. 'Oh, I'd forgotten about
that' he said 'I was hoping to go down to Devon to see my Dad
after his operation'. Mike's dad has had trouble with his knees for
ages and was finally going into hospital for a knee replacement
operation. Mike wanted to go down to visit him and check he was
okay. We couldn't both have the car so, mine being the shorter

journey, I agreed to check the train times. Whilst on the internet, battling to make sense of train ticket prices, I suddenly decided to check the weekend weather forecast on the BBC website. Fine and sunny all weekend, biking weather in fact. Why didn't I go to Leeds on my bike? That would be much more fun than waiting around in crowded train stations and sitting on hot, stuffy trains listening to people yelling 'I'm on the train' into their mobile phones. After all it was only about 100 miles and we had done 90 miles before breakfast before now.

'Mike, I'm thinking about going to Leeds on the bike' I said casually later that day. 'Your bike?' he said, looking confused. 'Yes, my motorbike, not my pushbike, you fool' I said, grinning at him, full of my own sense of daring. 'You are thinking of going all the way to Leeds on a 125?' he said in his Victor Meldrew 'I don't believe it' voice. Here we were again, in the border territory, but obviously Mike hadn't spotted this and so was happily pushing me over the 'I am definitely going to do this' line. 'Yes, why not? It'll be good practice before my Direct Access course next week' I replied, feeling more and more determined in the face of his disapproval. 'How are you going to get there? You can't ride on the motorway as a learner' he stated, matter of factly, as if the only roads that connect towns which are miles apart have six lanes and two hard shoulders. 'I will go over the tops, like I used to do years ago when I was at university and drove old bangers' I said defiantly. Without saying another word, Mike got up and went out to the car and came back with our tabloid sized road map. He laid it out on the coffee table and tracked down the relevant pages. 'So, show me which way you are thinking of going' he said pointing at the map. 'Well, first I'll go to Leek, then Buxton, then Chapel-en-le-Frith, then Glossop, then up into the Pennines. I'll stop at this reservoir, because there's a car park and some toilets there, and then I'll go over the tops to Barnsley, Wakefield and then Leeds. Easy.' I said, trying to sound more confident than I actually felt now that I could see the actual route in front of me. 'Well, I think you're mad trying to do it on a 125' he said, still studying the map. Wrong push. 'I'm not mad, it's a great idea, it'll be fun' I said. Sometimes I surprise myself with the things I decide to do.

I rang my mum to tell her what I was planning and as usual she had her own tales of adventure to tell. 'Oh, you'll love it. I used to do that journey on my Honda 90 when I was at uni 'she said wistfully. Yes, I remembered it now. When both my sister and I left home to go to university in the late 70's, my mum had just finished her pottery A level, passing with an A grade. Having left school with no qualifications and spent years working in all kinds of jobs from weaver, to delivery driver to artists model she had finally signed up for lots of correspondence courses and got herself some O levels. She then went to the college where my dad worked as a technician and did an A level in pottery. With us away, and only my teenage brother at home, she decided that she ought to carry on with her education and so got herself accepted onto a Fine Art degree in Leeds. However, this proved a little too esoteric for her so she switched to a Ceramics degree at Stoke. To do this she had left home, moved into student digs and become a full time student at the age of 40. No longer having access to the car, she bought herself a little Honda 90, which my brother taught her to ride on the local playing fields. She used this to get around Stoke at first, then started venturing further afield to come and stay with us for the weekend, and finally she began these regular mammoth journeys across the Pennines back home to see dad. 'I used to set off at dawn to avoid the traffic' she said 'and I used to take a flask with me and have a cup of tea at that same reservoir you're thinking of stopping at. It was wonderful watching the sun come up over that bit between Leek and Buxton' she mused. Right, that was definitely it, if she could do it on a Honda 90 I could definitely do it on a Yamaha 125. I said I'd see her around lunchtime on the Friday.

Mike left early on the Thursday morning, the day of his dad's operation, knowing that all further attempts to talk me out of this idea would be futile in the face of my mother's previous successes. 'You women' he muttered as he reversed off the drive. That evening I sat down to carefully work out my route. Again I had the problem of how to remember it, not the towns, which I could rattle off quite happily, but the road numbers. I decided to write them down on a piece of paper and then if they didn't come flooding back to me as I rode along I would stop and check my notes. Next I had to pack. What would I need? I had decided to take a rucksack that I would wear on my back so I didn't want it to be too heavy. I sorted out a bit of underwear, a couple of clean T shirts and a toiletries bag. I didn't need much and if the worst came to the worst I could always borrow some of mums clothes, though this was not my preferred option because I knew I would have to listen to comments from her like 'Here you ar' Jackie, try this on, it's always been too big and baggy on me'. Later that evening Mike rang to say his dad was a bit groggy but doing fine. I told him about my preparations and he reminded me to put my mobile phone on charge overnight, then said he'd ring me again in the morning.

'So, are you still going ahead with this trip to Leeds then?' he asked, early the next morning. 'Yes, of course I am, the weather forecast is good and it'll be fun' I replied trying to sound light and breezy about the whole thing when I fact I had butterflies as big as bats in my stomach. 'I'll ring you when I get there, so keep your mobile on' I instructed him before saying my quick goodbyes and ringing off. He had sounded tired and anxious and I was moved to think that he had been worrying about me all night. In fact, he was actually suffering from a hangover following a heavy night in the pub with his brother but I didn't find that out till later. I made myself some sandwiches then finished off my packing with a bottle of water, my purse and credit cards and my mobile phone. It was a beautiful morning and the sun was shining brightly as I wheeled the bike out of the garage. I had cleaned it the night before and there it stood gleaming on the drive. I went and got my rucksack and as soon as I put it on I knew it was too heavy to wear for the entire journey so I decided to try and strap it onto the pillion seat using a couple of those stretchy, bungee things. It fastened on best with the top of the bag pointing to the rear. 'I just hope those zips don't work their way open as I'm going along, it would be just my luck to leave a trail of toiletries and underwear right across the Pennines' I thought. I checked the oil, brake fluid and the tyre pressures and all were fine so I was ready to go. I pressed the starter button. Nothing. What? I tried again. Nothing. The bike wouldn't start. I couldn't believe it. 'You swine' I thought 'you know I'm going on a long trip and you just don't want to do it, do you? Hurm, too lazy for a long journey eh? Well it's not good enough. If you don't start now, that's it, I'm going to stop riding you and get something more reliable and then you won't get any journeys, will you, you'll be stuck in the garage all the time .. ha!' Fortunately, I wasn't thinking aloud so no one could hear this mad dialogue. I have a theory about machines and equipment which goes something along the lines, you buy them, you love them, they let you down, you hate them, you then settle into a more normal 'it's just a machine' kind of relationship with your new computer, car, fridge, phone, motorbike or whatever. It's just technology's way of reminding you that these things are fallible. I tried one more time and hey presto, it started. Obviously, my telepathic telling off had had some effect. By now I was sweating in my hot gear so I decided to get moving. I went and filled the bike up with petrol, all £3's worth, and headed out towards the Staffordshire Moorlands.

I rode along with a big grin on my face. I felt like Columbus setting out to find America which, I know, is ridiculous but when you spend most of your life chained to a desk, slaving over a hot computer, answering telephones, with the only breaks being short walks to the shops to buy something for tea, this kind of trip does feel like a real adventure. I'd just read a book of Hell-Raising Motorcycle Tales called 'Ridin' High, Livin' Free' by Ralph 'Sonny' Barger in which he says 'The main reasons people ride motorcycles are to clear their heads, feel the wind, and experience freedom'. Now I know I'm not a true biker in the sense that I don't belong to a chapter of the Hell's Angels, nor have I ridden miles in all kinds of weather. I haven't been riding bikes since I was knee high to a grasshopper and I have never been to a TT event or motorcycle race meeting or followed the careers and racing exploits of the great riders like Barry Sheene and Carl Fogarty. In fact, I know hardly anything about motorbikes and the people who ride them. Yet, whenever I am out on my motorbike I too experience that wonderful sense of freedom. So as I set out that morning I felt fantastic, I just felt so alive in the world.

About an hour later I was sure I was going to die. Heading out across the tops between Leek and Buxton the sky darkened and the wind picked up. I was beginning to feel really cold but worse still, the wind was buffeting the bike around. Then a big lorry went past me on the opposite side and I got the shock of my life as the bike was almost sucked across the road into oncoming traffic. Help! What should I do? Should I drop my speed? This didn't seem like a good idea because I was already struggling to do about 40 miles an hour and the cars that were overtaking me were also buffeting me around. Perhaps I should just stop and wait .. but for what? The wind could get worse and, by now the skies were so heavy I feared it might rain too. 'Better to try and keep moving' I thought. I pressed on, riding as far to the left as I dare whenever any lorries came towards me on the other side of the road. It was a nightmare. Just as I reached the plateau on the top and was beginning to think I might make it to Buxton in one piece, a huge lorry came up behind me. It had a big wind spoiler thing on the roof of the cab and looked as big as a house in my wing mirrors. Eeeeek! I knew that when it went past I would be riding in the middle of my own personal tornado. I would have cried but for the fact that all my bodily fluids had been diverted to the cold sweating department and there was nothing left for tears. Then a wonderful thing happened. The driver, who I am convinced must have been a biker himself, pulled back and slowed down and followed me slowly down the hill and into the town. His lorry gave me some protection from the wind and the turbulence caused by oncoming traffic so I was able to ride a bit quicker and a lot smoother. All the way down the hill I was thinking 'Thank you, thank you, thank you ..' willing him to hear my thoughts. What a life saver.

In spite of my harrowing ordeal I decided to press on and only stop at the reservoir because I knew if I did stop I would have to find a toilet. It's a psychological thing with me that whenever I break a journey I always have to go to the toilet, even if I only went half an hour ago. So I carried on. By now I was really feeling the cold. The sun, which had been so bright when I set off had now all but disappeared. My hands were cold in my summer gloves and I hadn't brought my thermal linings, what a fool. I only had a sleeveless T shirt on under my jacket and my arms and neck were getting cold too. My teeth were trying to chatter but the helmet prevented that so they had to settle for alternate grinding and clenching. I arrived at the reservoir and rode into the deserted car park. After a quick trip to the toilets I got my sandwiches out and ate my packed lunch, all the time hopping up and down to get warm and stretch my legs. I unpacked the one cardigan I had brought and put that on. As I stood there shivering, it suddenly occurred to me that it might rain and then I would really be in trouble, having no waterproofs with me. I could have kicked myself for being so unprepared, what was I thinking? Thank goodness Mike couldn't see me now.

I got back on the bike and set off over the tops to Barnsley. It was still cold and windy and there was a lot more traffic on the main Manchester to Barnsley road so I just got my head down and concentrated on riding as well as I could. In Barnsley the sun came out and it felt wonderful. 'At last' I thought 'a bit of heat to warm my aching bones'. Then all was going fine until I rode into the outskirts of Leeds where I realised that I was riding further and further forward on the bike. I was almost sitting on the petrol tank. Why was I doing this? I felt like one of those car drivers I sometimes see who drive with their faces right up to the front windscreen. I pulled into a bus lay-by to investigate and found that my rucksack was now half on my seat. It had slowly been squeezed up against my back and onto my seat by the bungee straps, a bit like the air in a long balloon when you squeeze it in the middle. As it had happened very gradually I hadn't noticed and had just kept moving forward slightly to compensate. No wonder I was sitting on the petrol tank! I spent a few minutes kneading it back into shape and was then off for the final lap. I eventually pulled onto mum's drive three and a half hours after I set off, grinning and shivering, a cold hen on a hot cruiser.

My mum was pacing the garden. 'Where've you been, I thought you'd be here by now' she said sounding almost angry. 'What? I've ridden like the clappers, it didn't take me that long, did it?' I said, wondering if I was now going to hear that she did it on her Honda 90 in something ridiculous like under two hours. 'I don't think it took me that long' she said. I knew it. 'Look, shut up, I'm here now and I'm freezing so get the kettle on'. She turned to go indoors then turned back and looked longingly at the bike. 'You did ever so well, ar' Jackie, and I'm glad you're here safe and sound. It's a lovely bike, isn't it? Now, if I'd had one of those ...' I was about to reply but, having switched on my mobile phone, I realised it was beeping and buzzing like a demented insect. I had an answerphone message from Mike 'Where are you, you should be there by now, ring me'. Oh he's worrying about me, that's nice I thought. I rang him and, feeling like I was speaking from the winner's podium, I told him all about my travels. Later that evening, after much rummaging in the attic, my mum presented me with a photograph of her and the Honda 90. 'Look, that was my little bike' she said proudly. In the picture she is sitting on the bike, stroking our dog Buster who has obviously run out to greet her. 'Is that a wicker basket on the back?' I asked, not sure I could believe what I was seeing. 'Oh yes, it was a sort of fisherman's basket that I rigged up on the back to put all my bits and pieces in' she replied matter of factly. I had to smile. I too have a wicker basket on the front of my bicycle. Mike calls it my 'Miss Marple bicycle'. She must have looked like Miss Marple on a motorbike, slogging her way over the Pennines on her little yellow Honda 90.

Up hill and down dale

A course was planned, and the next day at dawn they stood at the starting line. The hare yawned sleepily as the meek tortoise trudged slowly off. When the hare saw how painfully slow his rival was, he decided, half asleep on his feet, to have a quick nap. "Take your time!" he said. "I'll have forty winks and catch up with you in a minute."
The tortoise and the hare, Aesop's fables

The rest of the weekend was spent house hunting with Helen and James which was not easy as they were first time buyers, on low incomes, trying to find something they could afford in a happening city like Leeds. House prices seemed to be going up almost by the hour. We decided to try looking in Bradford too, as Helen worked there, and we found you could get a lot more for your money but I worried that she would be away from family who could help with the new baby. So nothing was decided, other than they would need to keep looking and I would have to come up again in the near future. As I was bemoaning the situation to my mum and dad later that evening the phone rang. It was Mike. 'I've just checked the weather forecast and it's going to be really nice tomorrow. How about I ride up and meet you at the reservoir? I can bring a picnic and then we can ride back together' he said sounding very keen and enthusiastic. What a lovely idea, it really cheered me up. 'Yes, great, I'll ring you when I set off because it's about half way and so we'll probably both need to leave about the same time' I replied, all excited.

The next morning I woke to glorious sunshine and started getting ready to leave. I was all giddy and excited about going to meet Mike, it felt like my first motorbiking 'date'! Mum looked at me as I gulped down a quick cup of coffee. 'How romantic, meeting your fella on his motorbike, I wish it was me' she said wistfully. It's hard for my mum, she is incredibly young at heart and active for her age and my dad, who is ten years older than her, has MS and is now more or less confined to a wheelchair. She is his carer and although she doesn't let this get her down, nevertheless her wings have been clipped in recent years. Mind you, sometimes she overestimates what she can do at her age and gets herself into some right pickles. 'Well I redesigned the garden at the bottom and needed some more top soil. I had seven tons delivered by accident, I only needed about two. It was a huge mountain of soil right up the side of the house, I thought it was going to bring the neighbours fence down. I had to get our Jon (my brother) and Terry (a family friend) to come round and help me barrow it down the garden. I managed to give about half of it away to neighbours and a builder friend of Jon's and then I had to raise all the beds in the front garden too to get rid of the last lot. I was shattered.'

Stories like this are not uncommon and fortunately I only get to hear about them after they have happened. So I dread to think what she would be up to on the motorbike front if she didn't have dad to worry about.

Anyway, I sorted the bike out, said my goodbyes and set off. The ride to the reservoir was lovely, except for trying to find my way through the road works in Barnsley city centre. Some towns seem to have very creative approaches to road diversions where they start you off with arrows and instructions and then leave you high and dry in the middle of some housing estate or, in Barnsley's case the one way system right in the middle of the shopping area. Riding round Wolverhampton the other week was a case in point. The main Penn road was closed and the signs said Road Closed, Follow Diversions, so we did and ended up in a tiny cul-de-sac with loads of other cars all doing U turns. I don't know why they don't just be honest and have a sign which says 'Road Closed, so make it up yourself from here'. Anyway I was making good time and enjoying myself and before I knew it I was riding into the car park at the reservoir. In contrast to my stop on Friday, the car park was packed and the main parking area on the right was full of motorbikes. Big sports bikes surrounded by big leather clad sports bikers. They were standing round admiring each other's machines and drinking mugs of tea from the mobile snack bar. As I tootled up the hill I panicked and thought 'I can't park up near them, I might wobble or stall or run into them or something and then I'll look a right fool' so I carried on up the hill to the higher levels. Unfortunately, access to the parking areas on the higher levels is over a cobbled trench that must be a water run off channel or something so I had to bounce and bump my way across this to park up amongst the cars. What was the matter with me? What was I thinking? Talk about uncool. I parked up and waited. Mike was nowhere to be seen. Then I noticed that the big bikers were getting ready to leave. I watched as they suited up, revved up and headed out of the car park. I waited a bit more. I was getting nervous. Was I going to be stood up? Then I heard the rumble of bikes and two gleaming Harley Davidsons cruised into the car park. Now they did look cool even if they were a bit noisy. Where was Mike? I was starting to worry again when in he rode, wearing his full biking gear including his frog's legs leather trousers. I skipped down the hill and waved him into the lower car park as it was now empty, apart from the Harleys. He parked up and grinning with a triumphant look on his face he said 'Where's your bike?' I explained and pointed to it and then went and brought my gear down before sitting on the bike and freewheeling it down the hill to rest next to his. I felt ecstatic. We had made it, both of us. The sun was shining and I was with my man, out on the motorbikes, 'it doesn't get much better than this' I thought. Mike was also feeling good but very hot and sweaty. He had decided to wear all his protective gear this being such a long journey for him but he was suffering for it now.

We settled down to eat the picnic that he had brought in his rucksack. 'That's a big bag for a few sandwiches' I said 'why didn't you bring your smaller, over the shoulder, one?' 'Well, I brought the road map too, in case I got lost' he replied, as he struggled to drag the massive, tabloid size road map out of his rucksack. I just burst out laughing because no matter how much Mike complains about my navigating he is hopeless at remembering routes and finding his way around unfamiliar places. 'What are you laughing at?' he asked looking hot and bothered. 'You with that massive map' I replied 'surely you didn't use that on the way up?' Then, in a 'look, it can't be helped' tone of voice, he explained that he had got a bit lost and he did have to stop once and get the map out and it was a nuisance and in any case we needed a smaller pocket sized map if we were going to go any distance on the bikes. He was right of course but that didn't stop me chuckling at the thought of him laying the map out on top of his bike like a picnic blanket. 'In any case, I thought we would go back a different way, you know, take in a bit of the countryside' he said as he studied the map. 'What do you mean?' I asked. 'Well I thought we could go back down to Glossop and then over Snake Pass to Ladybower reservoir and then down through Tideswell and Miller's Dale, then onto Ashbourne and home. It would be more interesting than just going back the way we came, what do you think?' He looked at me with a twinkle in his eye. I felt like a naughty school girl who had just been dared to do something slightly risky. 'Yes, why not, sounds good' I replied, trying to sound nonchalant, like I did this sort of thing every day of the week. As we started to pack up I decided to visit the loo one last time. On the way up to the toilet block I passed the Harley riders who were sitting round a table by the mobile snack bar, with their wives. The foursome, all older than me, looked jolly and friendly and, with their biking jackets hooked around the backs of their chairs, nothing like bikers apart from one of the men who had the obligatory long grey Harley rider's beard. The younger of the two men asked me, as I was passing, 'Is that a 125cc? It looks bigger than that.' He was looking at my little Virago as he spoke. 'Yes' I replied and then, keen to show off my biking skills, I explained about my weekend in Leeds and riding it there and now meeting Mike here at the reservoir. 'Very good' he said 'though I must say that when you brought it down the hill just now I thought to myself, my god, that bike's got a quiet engine'. Obviously he was referring to me freewheeling it down the hill, though it did cross my mind that almost any other make of bike must seem quiet to Harley riders. I told them about being too scared to park next to the speed bikers and so rode straight past them and parked up the hill. They all laughed and then the older man said it was all about confidence and riding experience. 'I know' I said, trying to sound like an old hand at all this 'I found riding in strong wind was really difficult, do you have trouble with the wind?' I asked. They all snorted with laughter before I realised what I had just said. 'Only riding with it, not in it' said the older man to guffaws of laughter from the rest of the group and a slap on the arm from his wife. We all had a good laugh and then they packed up and BUM, BUM, BUMMED their way out of the car park. Those Harley Davidson bikes are fantastic to look at, especially when they are kept so beautifully clean and shiny but boy, are they noisy. A few weeks later I came across a group for women bikers on the internet called Women in the Wind. It brought to mind that conversation by the reservoir and when I pointed it out to Mike he said 'Perhaps you could start your own group called Women with the Wind' a look of glee on his face. 'Do you mind' I said but it made me chuckle too.

So fed and watered and with everything repacked, we set off on our new route home and what a route it turned out to be. Back into Glossop where, with a speed bike right behind me, I made a mess of a tight left turn at the lights and ended up going wide. Fortunately the speed bike hung back till I repositioned myself correctly in the middle of the road, cheeks burning with embarrassment. Why does that always happen? When no one is watching me I can corner and turn and hill start beautifully but give me an audience and I can fluff it every time. Then we set off up Snake Pass. As we started the climb up the pass there were signs all along the roadside that had a picture of a leaning speed biker and the words 'TO DIE FOR? … RIDE SAFELY'. 'I need to watch my speed here' I thought to myself. Who was I kidding? Within minutes Mike had zoomed off up the hill, quickly followed by the speed biker who overtook me at the first opportunity, followed by a couple of cars obviously losing patience with my rapidly diminishing speed. As I dropped down through the gears I struggled to get much above 30 miles an hour. I began to feel like I was riding in slow motion then realised that I was riding in slow motion. 'C'mon, c'mon, you can do it, move, move' I chuntered to myself as I urged the bike up the hill. Then I realised I was on my own on the road, no cars in front and no cars behind so no pressure. Just me, the bike, a newly surfaced, smooth and even road and the most wonderful sun drenched scenery that I had seen in a long time. I relaxed and just decided to go with the flow, well more like trickle where my bike was concerned, but what did it matter? I knew Mike would wait for me at the other end because he would never remember the roads home so I just sat back and enjoyed the ride. It was marvellous, like riding through Switzerland with hills and valleys and trees and breathtaking views down to the reservoir. I felt so happy I found myself laughing out loud. Snake Pass is something else on a bike, on a warm sunny day with hardly any traffic. Fantastic.

As I had suspected, Mike was waiting for me in a lay-by halfway down the other side, a big grin on his face. He gave me the thumbs up sign and we set off again and made our way down through the dales. Many of the villages in the Derbyshire Dales are incredibly pretty clusters of lovely old stone cottages with hanging baskets, village greens and duck ponds, and it was a delight to slowly ride through them with our visors up, taking it all in. I don't remember enjoying seeing them this much through the windscreen of a car. On motorbikes you feel much more immersed into your surroundings, you see things more close up and you get all the smells of new mown grass and summer crops, as well as muck spreading of course. It all just feels somehow closer and more real. We stopped at Parsley Hay again for a cup of tea. Then we both did a terrible hill start getting out of there and onto the Ashbourne Road, we stopped briefly in Ashbourne for petrol and then finally made our way home. We pulled onto the drive, clambered off the bikes, removed our helmets and stood there dazed with exhilaration and exhaustion. We had spent almost six and half hours in the saddle, so to speak, covered about 140 miles and, in my case, spent another £3.50 on petrol. What a hoot! 140 miles might sound like nothing to those seasoned bikers who go to Scotland and back in a day but to us relative newcomers it felt like a major achievement. As we crashed on to the couch with a glass of wine we just kept looking at each other and laughing. 'So the Dales today and my Direct Access course tomorrow' I said nonchalantly. Mike raised his eyebrows, smiled weakly and said nothing which I put down to tiredness. As I made my way up to bed for an early night I thought to myself 'After all the biking I've done this weekend, the Direct Access course is going to be easy-peasy', little knowing that the following week was going to be one of the most tiring and difficult weeks I have ever had in my life.

Day one on a big bike

Whether you believe you can do a thing or not, you are right.
Henry Ford

The following morning I woke up feeling quite rested but nervous. It was like the CBT day all over again. 'I don't know why I'm so nervous' I said to Mike, between trips to the toilet. The weather was cool but promising to warm up so I decided to wear jeans and old men's socks with my biking jacket. If I wear ankle socks, my biking boots sometimes rub my leg half way up the calf so I prefer to wear long socks. However, for some reason it is almost impossible to buy knee high socks these days and when I asked the man on the sock stall in the market he looked at me, winked and said 'You mean school girl socks' and I knew he'd got the wrong idea. In the end, the only place I could find any was in Marks and Spencer's men's department and they were the long woolly ones that old men like to wear. What with my crew cut haircut and men's socks, not to mention my ruined nails from wearing riding gloves, I'm expecting a house call from the fashion police any day now.

Mike said he would run me up to the bike school and then come and collect me at lunchtime. I was booked in to do four, 3 hour sessions before my road test on the Friday. When we got to the school I was told that Danny, who was going to be my instructor for the day, had not arrived yet so I had to wait around for a while. This was the same Danny who thought I was a size 12 so I didn't mind waiting. I mean if he's the sort of bloke who says nice things about your dress size he might be the sort of bloke who would say nice things about your riding abilities even if they were complete rubbish and that was fine with me. Lots of positive encouragement, that's what I needed. I waited around, feeling more and more anxious. After my third trip to the loo I told myself to calm down and get a grip. Then Danny arrived and, after a quick hello and a brief chat about my riding experience so far, he took me outside to sort out a bike to ride. Four blue Kawasaki ER 500s were lined up on the car park. They reminded me of the donkeys I used to see on the beach when I was a kid, all lined up and ready to give rides. The bikes looked a bit like Mike's Honda CB 500 but without the aggressively hunched fuel tank. I felt my stomach knot up as I thought 'Well, at least they're a nice colour'. Danny suggested I take the one with the lowest seat and then he made me sit on it to check that I was happy with the riding position. Was I happy with the riding position? Not much, it was nothing like the cruiser position on my little Virago. Imagine sitting astride a plump Shetland pony in such a way that you could steer it by holding on to its ears, well, that was how the riding position felt to me. At least my foot controls were at the bottom of the engine and not half way up, so I didn't have to squat over the bike like a frog, like a lot of the sport bikers seem to have to do. Danny adjusted the clutch lever so that it was the right distance for my grip. Then he started explaining the controls to me. They were very similar to the ones on my own bike but I still couldn't stop myself from feeling incredibly anxious. Danny must have picked up on this because he looked at me and said 'What's the matter?' 'I'm just a bit nervous' I said with a weak smile. 'What are you nervous about?' he asked. 'Well .. the bike' I replied in a quiet voice, hating myself for sounding so weak and pathetic. 'What about the bike?' he asked, a puzzled look on his face. 'Well, I'm scared because this bike looks and feels so big and powerful compared to my little 125'. Danny laughed. 'Look Jackie, stop being so nervous, it's not that different to your bike and you've done, what, 2,000 miles on that one so you'll be fine on this one. It's not rocket science, just do what you do on your own bike till you get the feel of this one. Yes, you've got more power but you control that with the throttle'. I tried to look reassured but couldn't stop myself from blurting out 'But my feet only just reach the ground, what if I drop it?' Danny gave me a 'What is she like?' sort of look and said 'When you stop, your right foot should be over the rear brake so the bike will naturally lean slightly to the left which means your foot will be flat on the ground. If you drop it, you drop it, you won't be the first or the last to do that so stop worrying and get riding round the car park'. I realised that he'd twigged that I was a worry wart and so had decided to take a firm line with me. Before I could say another thing he turned the key, checked it was in neutral, pressed the starter button and the engine roared into life. Well, I say roared but actually it was more like a continuous loud snoring and grunting, rather like the noise in the pig pens when I used to

take the girls to the open day at the local Agricultural College.
'Go on, off you go' instructed Danny as he waited for me to get
started on slow manoeuvres. I put the bike into first gear, gave
it a few revs, which I immediately felt as vibrations through
the seat, and then slowly let out the clutch and started rolling
forward. I didn't kangaroo around the car park, or surge forward
or have to break sharply. I just rode around slowly in big circles.
Danny smiled and gave me the thumbs up and went back into the
office for something. I couldn't believe it, I was rumbling around
okay, albeit in first gear. All my slow riding practice around the
industrial estate seemed to be paying off as I remembered to
control the speed using the clutch and rear brake pedal. I was just
beginning to feel quite proud of myself when Danny came out
and put some cones out and signalled to me to ride around them
in a figure of eight. Here we go again I thought as I performed
wonderful figures of nine, six, zero and the occasional eight.
Then just when I thought my hand was going to seize up from
squeezing and releasing the clutch, Danny came out and signalled
to me to ride over and stop by him. 'Right Jackie, as this is your
first lesson what we're going to do is some general riding to see
how you get on. I want you to get used to the bike and how it
handles and if you're happy with it you can stick with this one for
your test. If you're not we've got time to change it and try some
of the others. We need to get the radio mics on because as we
ride around I'm going to be talking to you about observation till
you're sick of hearing me. You've been riding round here just fine
so we'll get ready and get out on the road. Okay?' He gave me a
reassuring smile whilst I nodded okay back to him, thinking 'Am
I okay? I haven't even been up into second gear on this thing yet'
but I decided to keep quiet and just concentrate on riding.

With the mics in place, Danny hopped onto one of the other Kawasakis and said, through my ear piece, 'Right Jackie, let's get moving'. I started to follow him out of the car park onto the long, winding stretch of road that runs through the industrial estate. As we picked up speed I knew I had to change gear so I flicked it up into second and gave it some throttle. The bike surged ahead and I jerked backwards. 'Whoooaaaa' I heard myself saying as I closed the throttle, like I was trying to rein in a stampeding horse. Danny was moving away and I could hear his voice calmly saying things like 'cars parked ahead, check mirror, then signal, look over the right shoulder and move out to go past them …' 'Get going you idiot' I said to myself through gritted teeth. So I rolled the throttle open and, yet again, felt like I was being catapulted forward, so I lost my nerve and let go of the throttle and slowed down. I clunked my way up through all the gears in this see-sawing manner. Stiff with tension, I couldn't believe how much power the bike had after the 125. A gentle turn of the wrist and the bike seemed to race forward, with me clinging on like a limpet on a torpedo. Whilst I floundered around with the gears and throttle Danny calmly sailed off into the distance, his disconnected voice mumbling in my ear 'check your mirrors, signal …' I made my way along the road in this lumpy, ragged fashion until I caught up with him at the junction with the main road. He seemed oblivious to my floundering incompetence, his voice droning on in my ear about checking to the left, looking over my shoulder, etc. I have to admit that I took heart from this, thinking my riding must look okay to someone watching it through a motorbike mirror. Either that or he was politely ignoring me whilst I tried to develop a smoother style of riding. We waited for a gap and then pulled out into the main road and set off towards the town. I began to get used to the extra power and the responsiveness of the throttle.

In my head I knew it was silly to be scared because I was in control of the speed, after all the throttle was in my hand but that still didn't stop me feeling like this machine had a mind of it's own and all I could do, when it started to race along, was cling on for dear life. It was funny really because I probably wasn't going any faster than I had on the Virago but my little bike had to be revved really hard to get any sort of acceleration whereas this bike just seemed to twist and go. Gradually I began to relax and my shoulder blades, which had been hunched up around my helmet, slowly dropped back into place and I could feel a draught on my neck again. I began to take notice of Danny's mutterings and tried to copy him. I was amazed at how much observation we were supposed to do. Roundabouts were a particular nightmare what with lane discipline, indicating, looking, road positioning, changing indicators, changing positions, looking in mirrors and life savers (which are the last look over the shoulder before you change direction). All this and ride the bike, it was exhausting.

At one point we rode along the road where we live and there was Mike going off to get a newspaper. As he heard the bikes he looked up and saw me. I waved to him as we rode past, trying to act nonchalant with a 'gosh, isn't this easy' kind of manner. It worked. He told me later that I looked incredibly at ease on the bike, so you see you can fool some of the people, some of the time. Danny then led me out of town into the surrounding countryside and onto some long open roads where the national speed limit applies. 'C'mon Jackie, the road is clear, let's get up to speed' he said, as he roared off ahead of me. I opened the throttle and thundered off after him. I began to feel really exhilarated. I had done 60 miles an hour on the Virago but only downhill with a good wind behind me and even then I knew that we were at the limit of what that little bike would do. This one, however, coasted along at 60 like this was a normal, every day kind of speed that it expected to do as a matter of course. I was thrilled, especially when it sailed up hills like they weren't even there. What a joy not to have to plan ahead for multiple gear changes to cope with any undulations in the landscape. We rode around for a while and then stopped on a disused car park to take a break and talk about how things were going. Danny told me that my general riding was fine but my observation and road positioning weren't too good. 'You tend to drift to the right, try and stay more central and also when you're turning you tend to signal, then look instead of looking in your mirrors first', I knew he was right but how did he know that? Surely he couldn't see whether I was looking in my mirrors or not? I asked him how he knew. 'Well, when I ride behind you I watch that little sticker on the back of your helmet and when it moves I know you're looking in your mirrors' he explained. 'I could just be moving my eyes and looking' I said, mischievously, whilst doing an impression of a pantomime villain's eyes as they check that the coast is clear. Danny laughed and then said 'You could, but you wouldn't see much because I've set the mirrors so that you have to move your head to see through them clearly, and you're not moving your head'. What? Surely that wasn't fair. If the mirrors were set differently maybe I could get away with sidelong glances. I challenged him on this. Danny looked at me calmly, 'Maybe you could get away with it, but this way I and, more importantly, the examiner will know that you're looking in your mirrors, which is what you have to do if you're going to pass your test. Though you should always be doing loads of looking anyway, test or no test, so do your observation Jackie'. I promised I'd work on my observation skills.

We rode through town with me trying very hard to do all my observation and failing quite a bit and then we rode back into one of the side roads in the industrial estate. Danny then explained to me that we were now going to practice the dreaded U turn. He talked me through it and then told me to get on with it. I did about twenty altogether of which about three were fine. I kept putting my foot down ('Foot down's a fail' said Danny's voice in my helmet) or, after tacking my way around, nearly running into the kerb ('Look where you want the bike to go. If you look straight ahead you will go straight ahead' said the talking helmet). It was so frustrating because this was the very road on which I had spent hours practicing U turns on my little Virago and I could do them fine on that. Once again I found myself deep in a mental argument with me. 'Look, concentrate, you can do this, what is the matter with you?' but all to no avail as I continued to grind and wobble my way around. Just as my hand was about to seize up with the strain of constantly squeezing the clutch lever, Danny called me over. 'Not bad for a first lesson but you'll need to practice that tomorrow. Now let's do some emergency stops'. My stomach knotted. Like most inexperienced riders I am scared of my front brakes. Images of the back wheel coming up and me flying over the handlebars come to mind, or the bike going into an uncontrollable skid before finally crashing over with me trapped underneath it. All very melodramatic I know, but my problem is I have a very powerful imagination. Danny talked me through it and then told me to go down to the end of the road, U turn and then ride towards him. When he raised his hand I was to do the emergency stop. 'What, you're going to stand in the middle of the road whilst I ride at you, are you mad?' I asked, incredulous. 'Yes, I will be in the middle of the road on the white line but you will be riding in the middle of your lane so not directly at me' Danny said with a 'C'mon, think about this' tone to his voice. 'Why can't you stand on the pavement over there' I pointed to a spot a safe distance away. 'Because I have to be able to see your foot on the rear brake pedal, to see if you apply it at the last minute'. Danny has to be one of the most patient people I have ever been around but even he was now wearing a 'stop asking all these questions and get on with it' look on his face. I rode off down the road, U turned (a good one actually) and then rode towards him, gripped with fear and desperate to see his hand go up. He raised his hand and I squeezed on the front brakes, the bike roared to a stop. I say roared because unfortunately when I pulled on the front brake lever I also accidently turned the throttle (they are both worked by the same hand) so there I was stood still on the road with the engine revving madly. Danny ran over and told me to close the throttle. I was shaky with adrenalin. 'I'm sorry Danny, but I couldn't bring myself to slam on the anchors 'cos I was scared of going over the handlebars' I wailed. Danny looked at me and laughed. 'No, that was fine, you stopped within the stopping distance' he said. I must have looked totally perplexed because he then said 'You do remember the stopping distances from your theory test, don't you? At 20 miles an hour you have to allow how many feet for stopping?' Stopping distances? Oh yes, of course I remembered them, they had taken me ages to learn, not to mention braking distances as well. Then suddenly a little light came on in my head. What had I been thinking? I didn't have to stop on a sixpence, I was allowed 40 feet to stop when travelling at 20 miles an hour. What an idiot. There was me thinking I had to stop, on the spot, the minute he raised his hand. 'One of these days I'm going to develop joined up thinking about all this' I thought to myself. So I did a couple more which went okay, and then we headed back to the school.

The last act of the day was to try and put the bike on the centre stand. Danny showed me how (there's a knack to doing this) and then I had a go. It was a real struggle but I managed it a couple of times. 'Why do we have to do this?' I whined 'my bike hasn't got a centre stand and I would ask Mike to do this for me if I had a bike that had one'. Danny pointed out that I might be asked to do it on my test so to stop worrying about it and just practice. Another bloke called Jim was also practising this alongside me. I grimaced at him and said 'Do you find this bit hard too?' and he replied 'Not really but I just want to make sure I can do it okay because I am off to do my test in a minute and it's the one thing I haven't practiced till now'. Danny, having now removed his biking gear, wandered over and said 'Has Mike still got the Honda?' I nodded as I grunted and heaved the bike up onto its stand. 'Why don't you practice on that tonight if you're worried?' Danny suggested. I said I might and then mentioned that Mike was thinking of selling the Honda as he fancied a change. Jim's ears pricked up at this and he asked me what sort of bike it was. 'Well, it's big and sort of greeny grey with yellow flashes; it's got this massive petrol tank ..' Danny rolled his eyes then said to Jim 'Have a word with Mark, he sold it to Mike and he can tell you more about it' obviously deciding that Jim wasn't going to get any useful information out of me. Just then Mike turned up and I introduced him to Jim so that they could talk about all that technical stuff that men like to talk about like bhps, torque and numbers of cylinders.

Whilst Mike arranged for Jim to come and see the bike I went to take off my biking jacket and drop it in the car. Having hardly noticed the weather at all up to this point I now realised that it was actually quite a hot day with bright sunshine. When I came to remove my padded biking jacket I found that I had been sweating so much I couldn't pull my arms out of the sleeves. As I wrestled with my gear, trying desperately to shrug off my jacket that was sticking to me like glue, I overheard Mike, now talking to Danny, saying 'I've just seen a Harley V Rod on the main road'. He sounded excited and buzzed by this. Danny said 'Oh yes, the V Rods, they're fantastic bikes'. Alarm bells started ringing in my head. 'Oh no, Mike doesn't need encouraging down this line of thinking' I thought, now thrashing wildly in an effort to turn the jacket inside out so that I could peel my arms out of it. I managed to drag it off and sling it in the car in disgust before marching over to interrupt this burgeoning V Rod fan club. 'Yes, they are nice to look at' I chipped in 'but horrendously expensive'. Danny looked at me with a dreamy look on his face and said 'I know, but I love mine'. Aaaaarrrrhhh. Mike's face lit up. 'You've got a V Rod?' 'Yes' said Danny 'I share it with Ian (the other instructor) and it's fantastic'. I groaned. 'What's the matter with you?' asked Mike with a sly smile on his face. He knew exactly what was the matter with me. He knew that I was appalled by the price of the V Rods and so didn't want him to even think about them and here he was talking to someone who not only liked them but owned one as well. 'Danny, don't encourage him, they cost too much' I said, trying to sound firm and commanding. 'Yes, they're expensive but life's short and hey, you've got to live a bit' he said, grinning at Mike. Before I could get in another word Danny turned to Mike and said 'You ought to book a test ride and see what you think. I can give you the Harley garage number if you want, just ask for Colin and tell him I said to ring'. This conversation was definitely going the wrong way and I realised that I would now have to tread very carefully if I was to avoid pushing him into the 'I am definitely going to do this' camp. 'Yep, good idea' I said 'that's the only way you'll really know if you like them' I said, straining to sound supportive and relaxed about the whole thing. 'Yes, I might just do that' said Mike following Danny into the office to get the Harley garage number. I knew then that I needed to go away and think carefully about my tactics for the battle that might lie ahead.

A bit of a speed nut

Speed provides the one genuinely modern pleasure
Aldous Huxley

The next morning, with me still feeling sickly and anxious, we set off up to the bike school again. At the traffic lights at the end of our road we found ourselves following a little sports bike, with full fairing and L plates, so it was obviously a 125. The bloke riding it was wobbling all over the place, doing hardly any observation and at one point was so close to the back of a car when it stopped to turn right that he had to walk the bike backwards before he could ride round the car on the inside. 'What do you bet that he's going to the bike school?' I asked Mike. We decided to stay behind him to try and protect him a bit from the following traffic. Sure enough, we pulled onto the bike school car park just after him. I thought to myself 'He needs to practice on that 125 a bit more if he wants to pass his test'. It turned out

I was having my lesson with him and he was called Gary. Our
instructor that day was Ian, the co-owner of the bike school, and
the V-Rod, and before we got on the bikes he sat us down to ask
us how our first lessons had gone and what, if anything we were
worried about. Gary began by saying that during his first lesson,
the day before, he had hit the kerb, dropped the bike and broken
the gear lever whilst doing a U turn and was now very nervous
about doing U turns. I was shocked. My U turns had been very
higgledy piggeldy but I had never come close to dropping the
bike. Ian told him not to worry because lots of people dropped the
bike, which was why we were paying for the lessons, to cover all
that sort of thing and he would make sure Gary did a good U turn
today. Lots of people dropped the bikes? 'Yikes' I thought 'I must
have just been lucky yesterday'. Then Ian asked me what I was
worried about. My natural reaction was to say 'Oh, everything'
but I decided to suppress this inclination and instead said 'Getting
the bike on the centre stand'. The night before I had followed
Danny's advice and tried to practice putting Mike's monster
Honda onto it's central stand and no matter how many times I
talked myself through the steps I could not budge it an inch. Mike
had patiently demonstrated it a few times which only served to
fuel my rage and frustration because he seemed to think that me
seeing him do it, would somehow miraculously enable me to do
it. Whilst he stood close by to catch the bike should I completely
lose my grip, I yelled at him 'This bike is hopeless, it's too big
and heavy and I'm not practicing with it' and then stomped off
into the house to sulk. The net result of all this was that I had now
convinced myself that I would never be able to put any bike on
it's centre stand and this would mean I would fail my test. Ian,
who has a lovely friendly face and is the sort of bloke who exudes
warmth and empathy, smiled at me and said 'Right, let's start with

the centre stand then'. So off we trooped outside. I chose the same bike as the day before and then stood by it as Ian explained again the procedure for getting the bike on the centre stand. 'Right Jackie, use your right foot to push down the centre stand and then feel for the 'knees' of the stand to be resting evenly on the ground. Now, hold onto the pillion handle on the back of the bike with your right hand, then push down on the stand with the muscles in your leg and lift the back of the bike with your right hand.' He made it sound so simple. I took a deep breath and pushed down. The bike lifted, wobbled a little but did not rock onto the centre stand. I groaned. 'Use the muscles in your leg Jackie' said Ian patiently. 'I haven't got any muscles in my leg, only cellulite' I muttered. Ian burst out laughing. 'Okay, have you got any muscles in your arms?' he asked me, grinning. 'Not much' I replied, feeling wimpish and pathetic. 'That's not a problem because it is not about strength it's about technique. Now, push down with your leg and pull up with your hand and let the bike rock backwards onto the stand' said Ian. The great thing about Ian is that he talks to you like there is never any doubt that you will be able to do what he is asking you to do. So I concentrated on helping the bike to rock back onto the stand and then suddenly I had done it. I stood there looking shocked and uncertain, thinking 'It must have been a fluke'. But no, I then managed to put the bike on and off the stand several times in a row. I felt ecstatic. Everyday after that I could get the bike on and off the centre stand but I never had another go with Mike's Honda.

Then, with our mics in place, and a trainee instructor called Kev bringing up the rear, we rode to the petrol station to fill up. Then we travelled in convoy to a nearby town where Gary was going to be taking his test. The bike school uses three test centres all within a twenty mile radius so the instructors like and take you to some of the areas you will ride around on your test day. On the way there we had to travel on a dual carriageway that only had very light traffic on it and I could hear Ian telling Gary to get up to speed. When we pulled up on the edge of a housing estate Ian quizzed us about speed limits. 'How fast can you go on a dual carriageway?' he asked. I suggested 70 miles an hour, then changed my mind and settled on 60. Gary wasn't sure and settled on 70. Ian pointed out that we should know this from our theory test. I started to argue with him, pointing out that one particular piece of dual carriageway has 60 signs all along it and speed cameras to get you if you exceed that limit. He then pointed out that where there are speed signs you follow them but if there are no speed signs you should know the speeds. He sounded disappointed in us and I felt like the classroom dunce for not remembering all this stuff. I really did need to start some joined up thinking with all this. Ian then talked to Gary about going too slow on the way over. He said that we would be expected to get up to speed on bigger roads. We had to stay safe but make progress. If we dawdled along fast roads cars would always try to pass us, even in busy traffic, so we had to keep up with the flow of the traffic.

Next we headed into a housing estate to practice slow riding and manoeuvres. As we entered the estate there were big 20 mile an hour signs so I tried to stick to that. Then I heard Ian's voice in my helmet saying 'Jackie, speed up a bit, we are now in a 30 mile an hour zone'. Are we? I thought. When next we stopped Ian asked me if I had seen the new speed sign. I admitted I hadn't. Then he told me to 'always look up at the junction, whenever you turn onto a new road there will be speed signs up at the junction, so always look up at the junction'. I began to wonder how I had managed all these years driving my car. As car drivers I think many of us are incredibly complacent about driving, we drive round half asleep most of the time. We sort of know the speed limits and roughly follow the rules of the road but I suspect most of us feel cocooned from the dangers whilst sitting in our heated cars with the radio on. We almost expect all the rules and signs and traffic management measures to keep us safe and so don't feel any real sense of responsibility for our own safety and the safety of other road users. I can even remember journeys where I have travelled from A to B and cannot remember passing through certain places, like I was sleep driving or something. On a motorbike, however, it is very different. You are fully aware of everything you do and everything that everyone else is doing. You try to read the road like a hawk and anticipate what all the other drivers around you are going to do. It is the only way to stay safe because lots of car drivers are pretty irresponsible and don't seem to have much respect for other road users. This is particularly noticeable when you ride motorbikes. I am a much better car driver since I have learnt to ride a bike and I am also much more sympathetic to bikers. In the past, when I was stuck in traffic on the motorway, I used to think that bikers weaving between the cars were a nuisance. Now, however, I think about how hard it is to crawl along in traffic squeezing a clutch lever endlessly till your hand feels like it will cease up; how hot the bike engines get when they just idle as many of them are air cooled; how hot and stuffy the riding gear gets when you are not moving; how cold and wet you can get if it is raining and so on. Bikes need to keep moving and if there is room for them to squeeze through the traffic, well why not? Also, if all the bikes were to stay in line, the queues would be that much longer so why not let them filter through? I now try and stay central to my lane so they can get past me at least.

Next we pulled into a quiet road and did some U turns. I did about twelve and only put my foot down on two of them so was pretty pleased with myself. Gary's were fine too. I think it helped him being out on a lesson with a woman as it was okay to be a bit nervous and just get on with the riding, with no other males around to stimulate his testosterone levels. My emergency stops were okay too. Finally we headed off to the dual carriageway that takes us back home. I was leading and so, mindful of Ian's talk with Gary about getting up to speed, I opened the throttle and zoomed off at the permitted 70 miles an hour. After all the slow riding and manoeuvres it felt fantastic to just blast down the road. The rest of the group seemed to drop back as I sailed away and I thought that maybe Gary was struggling to get up to speed again. Then I noticed that Ian was catching up on me fast and as we approached the first major roundabout he tucked in behind me and stayed close for the rest of the long ride back to the school. Kev was obviously pacing Gary.

As we pulled into the car park I noticed Mike was stood chatting to Danny again and thought that maybe tomorrow I would bring myself in the car, as the only sure way to stop these two putting their heads together to talk about V Rods. I parked the bike and went over to the car to start the usual struggle with my helmet and biking jacket. Once again the sweat was pouring off me and gluing the jacket to my arms and as I wrestled with the sleeves I was thinking that there must be an easier way to do this. Walking back towards the office I heard Mike ask Ian how I had got on with the lesson. Ian looked at Mike, and then at me and said

'She doesn't need a 535 ..' I had told him about my dream of moving up to a Virago 535. 'What do you mean?' I asked. 'Well, it probably won't be fast enough for you will it?' he replied with a half grin on his face. Mike butted in and laughingly said 'What, she's a speed nut is she?' Ian, who obviously couldn't decide whether he found this amusing or worrying, said 'Yes, just a bit'. It seemed that my blast on the dual carriageway had unnerved him, which is understandable as my safety was partly his responsibility for the duration of the lesson, but I was mortified. I wasn't a speed nut. How dare Mike suggest I was a speed nut. 'I was getting up to speed, you said we had to get up to speed' I spluttered. 'I know, that's why I didn't say anything to you but you were pushing it a bit' he said quietly. Looking back at it now I remember feeling really indignant, as if I had been unjustly accused of doing something that I had been told to do anyway. If I am honest though, I had scared myself a bit and one of the things you have to learn as a rider is to find your own speed limits and what you feel safe with. Okay, it's important to go with the flow of the traffic but you don't have to push yourself to be the fastest thing on the road. The limit might be 70 miles an hour but lots of the cars might only be doing 60 and if you feel comfortable at 60 then that's the speed you should do. It's a fine line between making progress and not holding up traffic and riding at the speeds that feel right for your level of experience. I had exceeded my experience speed limit and Ian had recognised this and was pointing it out. I went home feeling exhausted and confused. I spent the rest of the day mulling over the days lesson and describing every last thing to Mike who looked bored and weary but I made him listen because, well, I needed to get this stuff off my chest. Then I made him ask me questions about the effects of carrying pillion passengers. The school had given me a sheet of paper with the sort of questions you get asked on your test. 'Here, ask me these' I said, thrusting the paper towards him. 'Do I have to, I'm trying to relax here, can't you do that yourself?' he said as he tried to bury himself even deeper into his newspaper. 'No, it's not the same and in any case I can see the answers on the sheet' I replied, thinking how unsupportive he was being, though in fairness I can't remember him ever asking me to help him with any of these questions. Very reluctantly he read out the questions in his 'bored to death' voice and I struggled to remember all the stuff about pillion passengers affecting balance and handling and steering. That night I slept in the spare bed. 'What, you're not sleeping with me now?' said Mike sounding thoroughly fed up. 'Look, don't take it personally, I'm exhausted and I need to get a good night's sleep if I'm going to have any chance of getting through the rest of the week.' I fell asleep dreaming of U turns and speed limits and pillion passengers affecting tyre pressures.

Be nosy

What we see depends mainly on what we look for.
John Lubbock

The next morning I woke up feeling sick and anxious again and very, very tired. My neck and arms were aching so I took a couple of strong paracetamol to try and numb out the pain. In line with my new anti V Rod tactics I took myself off to the bike school and found a huge bloke with a shaven head, tattoos and a cigarette in his mouth waiting outside. I got chatting to him and found out he was called Cliff and he was going off to do his bike test that morning. He already looked like the stereotypical big mean biker so I was surprised to hear this. He then admitted to me that he had been riding bikes illegally for years but now had the money to buy a couple of good ones and didn't want to risk getting nicked and losing his license, so he decided to go legal. This meant he had to revert back to a 125 with L plates on it, which he hated.

What made it worse was that he owned a pub where one of the local biking clubs met. He smiled and said 'They're great big massive blokes, really nice people. You should see them, they come in all covered in leather and ask for a pint of orange juice!' He told me that he had managed to keep his bike test quiet but then his wife had told them all what he was doing and he was now the butt of endless jokes. He rolled his eyes and tutted as if to say 'What can you do?' and I thought to myself what a nice bloke he was. I asked him if he was nervous about the test and he said 'No, I'm going to treat it just like a normal day out on the bike'. I was impressed with his cool manner, knowing that I would never be able to do that on my test day. I found out later that Cliff passed his test, no problems. Yes!

I was then told that I was going out with Ian again so I made a mental note to watch my speed and try to ride not too fast and not too slow. I was being paired up with a young woman rider who had done her CBT a couple of years ago and had been riding a little Honda 125, albeit intermittently, since then. She now wanted to take her test on her Honda and was then planning to ride that for the two years needed to qualify for something bigger. I sat chatting to her and found out that she had not been at all happy with the CBT course she had done in the neighbouring county. She told me that the course had only lasted just over half a day and when she finished it and was passed she was amazed, as she had made such a hash of her practical riding. They had then invited her back to do her Direct Access and she had declined feeling nervous and unhappy about riding motorbikes at all. However, she had persevered and got herself the little bike and ridden up and down her parent's driveway until she gained the necessary skills and confidence to go out on the road. Now that her CBT was running out she had decided to try and do her test on the 125 as she didn't feel good enough or strong enough to handle a big bike. As we were about the same height and build I did think to challenge her on this but then decided against it thinking that everyone has to choose the route that suits them. Michelle then went on to tell me that, following a recommendation from a friend to try this bike school, she was amazed at how thorough the training was here. She said that at last she felt like she was learning how to ride properly. I suppose standards can vary so I was just very pleased that by luck we had this very good school right on our doorstep. Danny and Ian pride themselves on producing competent and safe riders, in fact, they bang on about safety all the time but I suspect I would too if I was responsible for letting someone loose on a powerful machine that, if they weren't careful, they could then use to kill themselves. As Michelle and I sat chatting Ian came over and caught the end of our conversation in which I was saying that my plan, if I failed my test on the big bike on Friday, was to do what she was doing and retake it on my 125 and then ride that for two years until I qualified for something bigger. Ian looked aghast but said nothing. I took this as a good sign because it seemed to suggest that he thought I was capable of passing my test on the big bike.

We spent the morning riding around the town dealing with speed humps, road works, traffic lights and roundabouts. It was very hot and tiring. We then went to do some hill starts on a really steep hill just on the edge of town. Ian was picking us up on observation endlessly with comments like 'A lifesaver would be nice Jackie' and 'It's no good looking now, you're already turning' and a favourite of his which was repeated every time we passed through crossroads and by busy junctions, 'Be nosy, look into the junctions, even though you have right of way some twit might just decide to pull out on you'. When we stopped for a break at a local bike dealers (where Ian was greeted like a long lost friend and offered a place on a boy's night out to a lap dancing club!) I asked him if all this being nosy was really necessary. He said 'Yes, even if another motorist doesn't pull out on you, an emergency vehicle might come down the wrong side of a road or go round other cars to get through and you might not hear it with the noise of the bike and the helmet. Be nosy Jackie'. When it came to time to do my U turns and emergency stops I was feeling incredibly tired and made quite a hash of some of them. I tried to analyse where I was going wrong and talk through the various stages of each procedure with Ian but he told me not to think about it so much and just do it. Michelle was also struggling a bit but slowly improving with each successful attempt. As we made our way back towards the bike school we got stuck in traffic around some road works. We sat there, the bikes getting hotter and hotter as we crawled slowly along. My clutch hand was killing me and Ian must have noticed because his voice in my helmet said 'Jackie, put it into neutral for a bit and rest your hand until we start to move again. You shouldn't really but this looks like being a bit of a wait'. I was separated from Ian and Michelle by a yellow sports car with two young women in it. When the lights in the distance changed and we got ready to crawl forward the car pulled alongside me, crowding me towards the pavement. The driver obviously thought that if she pushed past me she would get ahead in the queue and have more chance of getting through the lights but what about my space on the road? I was just trying to decide whether I should pull over and let her take my place when Ian rode up and tapped on her window. I watched in my mirror as he lifted up the front of his helmet and said a few words to her, obviously telling her to get back and wait her turn. When the traffic moved off slowly she waited and I regained my place in the queue. Why do people do that? It's not as though she couldn't see me, on a big blue motorbike, wearing a silver helmet and a fluorescent waistcoat with the words RIDER UNDER INSTRUCTION splashed all over the back. We eventually rolled back into the bike school car park and parked up, tired but both feeling quite pleased with our riding, especially when Ian said we had done well and we were well on the way to being good riders. Apart from my U turns and emergency stops, I felt that I had definitely ridden much better than the previous day so perhaps in my last lesson tomorrow everything would come together and I would, like Cliff, be able to treat it as a normal day out on the bike. How wrong can you be?

The dreaded U turn

The lady's not for turning.
Margaret Thatcher

The next morning I woke up exhausted, having slept badly. I had spent most of the night reading the latest Harry Potter book to try and put all thoughts of my impending road test out of my mind. The only trouble was, in the story poor old Harry, Ron and Hermione were getting all worked up and nervous about their impending OWL exams (Ordinary Wizarding Levels) which only served to remind me of what was coming on the Friday. The only thing that kept me going was the thought that this would all soon be over – pass or fail, so I dragged myself out of bed and, continuing the policy of disrupting the V Rod fan club, I drove myself up to the bike school. It had been raining hard all night and was still raining when I was told that I was going out with Mark that day. You might remember Mark, the tall blonde Adonis of a bloke who had sold Mike his Honda. I went over to say Hi and he mumbled 'Hi' back to me. I said 'You sound bright and cheerful this morning' and he looked at me funny. My attempts at sarcasm never quite work, I can't seem to get the right tone to my voice so people assume that I'm being serious. It's something to do with coming from Yorkshire. Yorkshire people are hopeless at sarcasm because if they have any critical comments to make they just make them ('You're a grumpy old sod this morning'). They don't try to be clever and disguise their opinions in sarcastic opposites. When I first moved to the Midlands I was forever getting lost in conversations that were riddled with sarcasm as I didn't really understand it as a concept. Then over the years I began to try and do it a bit myself but never with much success. This was another unsuccessful attempt on my part so I had to backtrack and say 'Only kidding, you sound grumpy'. He looked a bit sheepish and admitted that he had ridden to London the night before to watch a band he knows play in a concert. Apparently he taught the lead singer to ride a motorbike and got him through his test so he has a standing invite to all their concerts when they are over here from America. So he had ridden down and back the previous evening, about 350 miles in total! I was stunned. Was he mad? I had heard of people doing 400 miles in a day but 350 miles in an evening, after being at work all day, well that has to be some kind of insanity. He looked nonplussed and said that it was no big deal. Nevertheless he did look tired.

He told me, and another bloke called Stewart who was coming on the lesson too, to get kitted up and ready to go. Stewart was nice, big, hunky and with two metal teeth like Jaws in the James Bond movie The Spy who loved me. I thought to myself 'Oh no, I bet he rides really well, he looks like a real biker and I'll be the dunce in the pack as usual' but he told me that he'd been riding an automatic scooter so was really nervous about using gears. Which just goes to show that you can't judge a book by it's cover. He was really nice and had only had one lesson so far and was as nervous as me. Out in the car park Mark asked me which bike I wanted and I told him that I thought they were all clunky and horrible but I usually had the one with the lowest seat. Then he asked me how I had been getting on with my U turns and I admitted that they were a bit mixed so he suggested I try riding a different bike. He said to me 'This bike is the newest one so it's the least clunky of the lot and the seat is a bit higher and I find that U turns are easier to do if you're a bit higher up. You can see what you're doing better and you're more on top of the bike so they're easier to turn. Have a go with this one, round the car park and see what you think.' So, reluctantly, I got on the higher bike and set off round the car park. He was right of course. Turning was a bit easier and the bike was less clunky so I opted to stay on that one. So off we went with Mark leading, me, then Stewart and Kev the trainee instructor bringing up the rear. As we headed towards the petrol station the rain fell steadily. Fortunately I had put on my biking trousers as well as the jacket so it was not too bad and the other three had waterproofs on too. As we filled up with petrol I asked Mark if we were going to the town where I was taking my test as I hadn't done any riding there yet. He said 'Okay' but he sounded very reluctant. I decided to press him on this and find out what was bothering him. 'What? What's the problem with going there?' I asked. 'Well, it's quite a long ride so we'll have to spend most of the lesson getting there and back and if the weather stays like this we're all going to get soaked and we'll be a long way from base. If we stayed around here we could always nip back for a cup of tea and a warm if it gets really horrible.' I could see his point but I could also feel my anxiety levels rising at the thought of taking my bike test in a town that I had never ridden in before. Mark obviously sensed my concerns and went on to say 'Look, back at the office I have a map of the town which shows all the different speed limits and obstacles. I could talk you through all those, give you the map and you could drive over later this afternoon and take a look. That way we can use this lesson to work on slow manoeuvres and not waste loads of time on straight road riding, which you can do okay anyway.' Reluctantly I agreed and we set off around the town. After about half an hour I wished I had insisted that we go to the test town because, at least then I would have done some easy road riding. Mark picked me up on everything. 'Jackie, you've got your test tomorrow, you're looking is just not good enough. Get your chin on your shoulder when you look back. It's no good just turning your head slightly one way or the other, you have to really look behind you' and 'Jackie, if you're turning left, get right over to the left so that it's clear to cars behind you what you're going to do' and 'Jackie, watch where you pull up at the side of the road, you were a bit too close to that parked car' and 'Jackie, when you push the bike across the road get it on full lock to make sure it goes round' and so on. His voice droned on in my helmet like some sort of army drill sergeant. The only thing that stopped me from packing up for the day was hearing that Stewart was getting the same sort of drilling. When we eventually pulled up at the back of a quiet housing estate to do our U turns and emergency stops I was feeling exhausted and dispirited. My U turns were hopeless. Mark came over and told me to get off the bike. 'Let me show you what to do and I'll talk it through as I go around'. As I watched him make two perfect U turns I almost burst into tears. My own voice in my head was wailing 'I can't do this, I am never going to be able to do this' but I knew I had to get a grip and not cry in front of the rest of them. I got back on the bike and started again. This time I listened carefully to what Mark was saying. 'Jackie, as you look back to check it's clear to turn, keep your head there and start the turn. Then you're already looking at where you want to go, so turn, unless there is anything coming of course.' So I started trying to do this. The temptation to always look forward is enormous but, he was right, if I looked back and then kept my head back I did start to turn. I was concentrating hard on doing this but his voice kept droning on in my helmet. Suddenly, I couldn't take it anymore. I pulled up alongside him, pulled up my visor and said 'Look, shut up, I need to think about how I'm doing this and your going on and on is putting me off, so shut up.' Mark looked shocked. I don't think anyone had told him to shut up before. Then a big grin lit up his face and he said 'Okay, see how you get on'. I set off again and did another lousy turn. I looked at Mark and shrugged my shoulders and his voice in my helmet said 'I'm saying nothing'. Slowly my turns got a bit better. Then we started on emergency stops and where my U turns had been hopeless, my emergency stops were a disaster. I just couldn't do the 'front brake, back brake, clutch in, stop' routine. I just pulled everything on and hoped for the best. Mark was onto me again. 'Look Jackie, pull the front brake on first, this forces the weight of the bike onto the front forks and so puts more power into the braking. Don't pull the clutch in until right near the end because you need the engine to drive down the front forks, otherwise you're just freewheeling and the bike is a lot less stable'. Then finally, 'Use the rear brake to lock down the back end.' I think that was what he said. All I can remember trying to do is 'front brake, forks down, rear brake, clutch' but as soon as he raised his hand I did 'front brakes, stoooooooopppp', much to his disgust. After several poor attempts I decided to pack in. I pulled up alongside Mark and stopped the bike. I got off and took off my helmet. He looked at me oddly as if to say 'What's the problem now?' I said 'I'm not doing any more of those today, I'm too exhausted and this is doing nothing for my confidence so I'm just going to pack it in and hope for the best.' Mark looked taken aback. I don't think he was used to having such stroppy students. 'You should keep doing them till you get it right' he pointed out. 'I know' I replied wearily 'but I'm not going to because I am not going to get it right today and all that this is going to do is destroy the tiny bit of confidence I have got, so I'm packing in now'. Mark looked at me for a moment with a calculating look in his eye, obviously trying to decide whether he could order me back onto the bike. I gave him a false grin, one where your mouth smiles but nothing else does, just so he would know I meant business. I was not doing any more U turns or emergency stops. He looked straight at me with a 'disappointed in you' expression on his face and I thought to myself 'I'd hate this guy if he didn't have such nice blue eyes'. Thinking this I couldn't help but smile at him. He grinned and shook his head in a 'What is this woman like?' sort of way. 'You're general riding is fine, you just need to think through some of the manoeuvres a bit more'. I pointed out that Ian had told me not to think too much and to just ride instead. Mark said 'He was saying that to get your confidence levels up on the bigger bike and your general riding is fine, but now we have to fine tune everything for the test.' 'Fine tune everything?' I said, 'more like scrap it and start again'. Mark laughed. 'Oh stop it, you'll be fine' and as he said this I heard a loud bang and looked round to see Stewart leaping away from the bike which he had dropped whilst doing a U turn under Kev's watchful eye. Seeing this, I hate to admit it, made me feel better because no matter how rubbish my riding was at least I hadn't dropped the bike, yet. Then, as we rode back to the test centre, I could hear Mark's voice in my helmet saying things like 'Don't forget, if it's raining tomorrow try not to ride over wet manhole covers and give yourself more stopping distance for the emergency stop' and so on. There seemed to be so much to remember when riding in dry weather conditions, never mind adding on lots of other things when it was raining. Once back at the bike school Mark told me to go through to the training room so we could look at his hand drawn map of the town where my test was going to be the following morning. We sat huddled together for about twenty minutes going over the various road junctions and speed limits whilst he ate his packed lunch. I did know the town a little but not enough to feel confident about riding around it on the bike. As I got up to leave, thinking 'tomorrow is going to be a disaster', Mark, obviously sensing my sombre mood, called after me 'You'll be fine, I know a place on the way to the test centre where we can practice your U turns before the test'. I looked back to see him grinning and thought to myself 'Oh no, I'm not going with Mark am I?'. 'Are you taking me then, to the test, in the morning?' I asked wearily, wondering whether I would be able to face another day with such a taskmaster. 'I don't know, do you want me to check?' he replied, a small smile playing across his lips. He reminded me of our cat, Toby, and the look he gets on his face when he is in the middle of playfully torturing some small furry creature he's caught. 'No, you don't need to check but if it is you taking me then you're not to give me a hard time, okay? I'm going to do my best but there's no point you giving me a load of stick in the morning because whatever you say, I can only do what I can do' I retorted snappily, obviously feeling the pressure. Mark just grinned and got back to his sandwiches. As I headed out of the door, a woman standing in the outer office said to me 'Is he your husband then?' nodding in Mark's direction. 'No, he's one of the instructors' I replied and she looked a bit taken aback. Obviously, Mark wasn't the only person unused to seeing cantankerous students.

I drove myself home to find a card waiting for me on the mantelpiece. It was a Good Luck card from Anne and Norman in which they had written 'Good luck with your test – we know you can do it!' I burst into tears. I couldn't believe it, what was the matter with me? And then I realised that I was exhausted and that day's lesson had been a nightmare leaving me feeling totally despondent. 'I wish I knew I could do it' I sobbed, full of self-pity. After five minutes of crying and quietly moaning 'Why am I doing this?' and 'What possessed me to want to put myself through this?' I decided enough was enough. I had started this of my own free will and I was going to finish it, and in any case, it would all be over by this time tomorrow so I might as well shut up and get on with it. I blew my nose, had a shower and went to bed for half an hour, hoping this would revive my flagging spirits enough to enable me to get on with the final task of the day, the reconnoiter of the test town. After a quick sandwich and a cup of tea, I set off with Mark's map spread out on the car passenger seat. I drove over to the town and, starting at the test centre, I slowly worked my way around it, comparing actual road signs with the signs on Mark's map. I drove into the road where Mark thought I might do my U turn and thought 'This isn't too bad, it's nice and wide and open on one side so that should be okay'. I went round all the roundabouts I could find and checked out how the lanes were marked on the road and finally I tootled round the housing estate where a lot of the slow driving usually takes place.

I felt better for doing this thinking that at least now I was familiar with the sort of roads I would be riding.

I made my weary way home, only to find Mike giving the Honda the clean of it's life. I had forgotten that Jim was coming over with a friend to take a look at it with a view to buying it. Mike said 'Jim rang earlier to say he is definitely coming over tonight. By the way, he failed his test the other day. He sounded a bit fed up but he's put straight in for it again and he still wants to see the bike'. Mike didn't sound surprised, as he had failed first time, and now that I was near the end of my course I wasn't surprised either. Riding motorbikes was harder than it looked. As we ate tea I told Mike all about my day and how horrible it had been and he listened and nodded. At least I think he listened, he looked like he was listening but this tale of woe had been going on for days now and so I suspect he was doing that male thing where they look like they are listening but they are, in fact, thinking about something entirely different. As I didn't really want him to say anything in response this suited me too and I just got on with having a really good moan.

Then Jim turned up with his friend so I tried to put on a brave face. 'Hi Jim, sorry to hear you failed your test the other day, what happened?' I asked. Jim gave me a blow by blow account of his test and explained that his biggest fault was riding onto a roundabout when a car was coming. The examiner said the car driver had been forced to slow down and this was a serious fault under the 'Judgment – crossing traffic' heading. Jim's friend said 'You can't win. If you see a gap and go for it you're being reckless but if you err on the side of caution they can get you for undue hesitation.' After a bit more discussion in which all three men agreed that you never pass first time anyway, Jim turned to me and said 'So when have you got your test then?' 'Tomorrow morning' I replied, now feeling totally dispiritied. Jim grinned sheepishly and said 'Oh well, good luck, I'm sure you'll be fine' and I wondered if, in fact, I had completely misheard the preceding conversation. The three of them then went off to look at the bike in the garage and talk technicals. Jim's mate had a Honda Hornet, which he loved and he seemed very impressed with the condition Mike's bike was in and recommended to Jim that he buy it. So a deal was struck and Jim said he would sort out the money and arrange to come and collect the bike the following week. When they left I telephoned my mum to ask her to do a spell for me. My daughter is not the only witch in the family. When she picked up the phone I said 'Hi mum, only me.' I must have sounded fed up because she instantly said 'Oh hello love, what's the matter? Is everything okay?' I explained about the test the following morning and asked her to do me a spell to help me pass. My mum has been doing this for years and although most of the family think it is a bit silly nevertheless any big tests or events and we all ring her up for one of her spells. I suppose it is bit like a good luck charm thing, a sort of new age alternative to a prayer. She got into this when she was studying Tarot cards, dousing and Reiki healing. Anyway I'm not sure what she does other than light a candle and ask for success for us but it always feels nice to know someone else out there is routing for you. She said she would see what she could do. Later that evening as I tried to relax in a hot bath, Mike brought me up a cup of tea and said 'Jim's put in for his test again but he couldn't get a date until next month and it's costing him another £100 so you've just got to get this test passed tomorrow'. 'So, no pressure there then' I thought as I sank down into the bubbles.

The big test

Celebrate good times, come on! Let's celebrate.
Kool & The Gang

On the day of the test I woke to clear blue skies, which was a relief as I had been kept awake some of the night by the sound of torrential rain drumming on the bedroom window and the rumble and crack of thunder and lightning. In addition to feeling tired and achy I was also feeling sick with nervous anxiety. I kept asking myself what on earth had possessed me to try and do all this in one week. I took some strong paracetamol before putting all my biking gear in the car. I would decide whether to wear full wet weather gear when I got to the bike school. Mike asked me if I wanted him to drive me there but I declined his offer. My test was at 10:45 and I wasn't sure what time I would get back. He came to see me off at the car and, giving me a big hug, he said 'Just do your best. You're a good rider and you've done loads more riding than I had when I did my test so I'm sure you'll be fine. Just show them what you can do'. I felt a lump in my throat. What a nice thing to say. I was just about to thank him for having such faith in me when he went on to say 'Besides which, you need to pass this test, because I am fed up of waiting for you whilst you struggle up the hills on that silly little bike of yours.' That silly little bike! How dare he, I loved that bike and in any case I was doing this test for me, not him, and he didn't have to wait that often as I usually managed to keep up most of the time. I was about to tackle him about all this but then I decided to save my energy for the test. Once I had checked that I had all the necessary documents with me I got in the car, smiled weakly at Mike and drove off to the bike school.

When I arrived Mark was getting the bikes out of the garage. He looked at me and grinned and it was then that I guessed that he was taking me to the test centre. I mumbled 'Morning' and stood waiting for him to confirm that my suspicions were right. He continued sorting the bikes out, lining them up and getting them going so that they would be warmed up and ready for use. I just stood watching, saying nothing and looking glum. I was struck dumb by nerves, which is very unusual for me as I can usually talk for England. Mark came over and said 'I'm taking you for your test so if you want to get yourself sorted out we can head off over there. What do you want to do in the hour or so beforehand?' I thought about this for a minute and said 'Go home and crawl into bed and sleep?' Mark looked at me to see if I was joking but then realised that I wasn't so said, his voice dripping with sarcasm 'You're not tired are you, you've only just got up?'. I decided to do the Yorkshire thing and take his statement at face value. 'I am tired. This week has been very hard work. I don't know why I let myself be talked into doing the course and the test all in one week'. Just as I said this Danny came walking across the car park and heard my comment. He piped up 'It was your choice. You wanted to do it all in one week, you said you wanted to get it all over in one fell swoop'. I looked at Danny in amazement. 'I don't remember saying that' I snapped. 'Well you did. Anyway stop moaning and get on with it, you'll be fine' Danny countered, a big grin on his face. I was about to argue this out with him and then thought 'No Danny is right, I need to shut up and get it over with'. However I couldn't resist saying 'You're not making me go for my test with him are you', nodding towards Mark, 'he's a right slave driver, he picked me up on everything yesterday, I went home with a headache!' Mark looked shocked but Danny didn't bat an eyelid. 'If he picked you up on everything you obviously needed telling so you should do fine on your test today. Of course, if you pass it will all be thanks to that first lesson with me when I got you off to an excellent start. If, on the other hand, you fail, it will be Mark's fault'. Mark snorted at this and I had to chuckle at Danny's cheek. As Danny wandered off Mark began to get us organised for the morning. Bikes were sorted and my paperwork checked. I asked him whether I should wear wet weather gear and as the sky was clear and it looked like it might be a fine morning we spent a minute or two trying to decide what was best. In the end Mark said 'Look, I'll take a rucksack and carry your biking trousers and a spare set of waterproofs so if you need to change you'll have something with you'. He also offered to carry my various bits of paperwork. It suddenly occurred to me that Mark was being quite supportive towards me. Perhaps my comments about him being a slave driver had hit a nerve and he was now trying to take a slightly softer line with me. Once we had

all the gear sorted and our mics on and working, Mark asked me
'Did you go over there yesterday and have a look round?' I told
him that I had and that his map was quite good and it did help to
see the roads. Then he said 'It's your morning, how do you want
to use the time?' I just looked at him blank. I had no idea. 'Look,
how about we ride across and, on the way, I know a quiet spot
where we can do a few U turns to get you warmed up and maybe
an emergency stop or two just to get you in the mood. Then I
could lead and take you round some of the roads that have given
some of our other students' problems in the last couple of weeks.
I want to show you some speed signs around a set of road works
that have caught a few people out. What do you think?' he said,
sounding concerned and friendly. What did I think? Not much.
I was pretty much past thinking and more into just functioning.
'Yes, whatever' I replied, totally unable to muster any enthusiasm
for the coming trial. Mark just smiled and realising that nothing
he could say was going to raise my morale, went over and got on
his bike and then signalled to me to move off.

We rode along saying nothing. I wasn't fooled though and every
time I missed an observation or fluffed a gear change I knew that
he knew but wasn't saying anything. He had obviously decided
not to put me under too much pressure. It was funny though
because in a way I wanted him to comment, if only to confirm
what I knew to be mistakes. After about half an hour of straight
riding we pulled onto a very quiet road on an almost deserted
industrial estate. 'Right Jackie, U turns please'. I groaned but
talked myself through the procedure and then did one of the
worst U turns I have ever done in my life. As I screeched to a
halt just as my front tyre bumped into the kerb I was shocked. I
was never normally this bad. In my helmet I heard Mark's voice

saying 'What are you doing?' I wasn't sure what I was doing.
Mark came over and started reminding me of what I needed to
do. I tried to listen to him but all I could hear in my head was
my voice saying 'I'm going to fail, I know I am'. I had another
go with a bit more success but it still wasn't good enough. I told
Mark I didn't want to do anymore and when he began to protest
I reminded him that it was my morning and I could decide how
I wanted to spend the time and I didn't want to spend it doing
poor U turns. 'Okay, well just do an emergency stop so that the
procedure is fresh in your mind' he said, walking off to position
himself by the road where he could raise his hand and see my
rear brake pedal. My emergency stop was also a bit ropey so I
did a few more, slightly better ones, and then decide enough was
enough. Whilst Mark was getting his helmet on and not watching
me I decided to just go round in circles doing U turns away from
his watchful eye and, would you believe it, they were all nearly
perfect. 'Typical' I thought ' when no-one is watching I can do
them fine'. We then road over to the test town and Mark led me
around a few roads pointing out obstacles and things to watch out
for on the test. In particular, he took me up a dual carriageway
that had road works on it and pointed out a speed sign that said 30
miles an hour, ¾ of a mile ahead. 'Jackie, don't drop your speed
at this point, as it's telling you the speed drops further on. One
bloke failed for dropping his speed here'. I groaned. I was never
going to remember all this. Eventually we pulled into the test
centre car park and parked up alongside two other bikes. Standing
next to them was a big bloke a bit like Cliff, the illegal biker, and
a woman with a fluorescent tabard with the word INSTRUCTOR
printed across the back. They were stood chatting and smoking
and looking well pleased with themselves. 'Oh no' I thought
'I bet he's just passed. Just my luck. Why couldn't I follow a

bad rider?' Mark took off his helmet and said hello to them and then explained to me that he was going to move my bike into another part of the car park where I would collect it for my test. I nodded and tried to smile but the nerves that connected my face muscles to my brain didn't seem to be working. 'Jackie, go into the test centre. There's a room on the right, just sit in there and I will come in and join you in a minute' Mark said in a quiet but authoritative voice. I nodded and did as he said. Once in the centre I looked around and quickly found the toilet. For some reason when I am extremely nervous I can't stop going to the loo and this was no exception. Back in the waiting room I sat on a chair and tried to read the posters on the walls and act cool and calm. Mark came in, took off his jacket and sat down. 'I've just been talking to the last lot and apparently the examiner today is following you round in a car and not on a bike.' It took a minute for this to sink in. 'What?' I said, unsure what I was supposed to think about this piece of news. 'Look, don't worry, in some ways it's better because it is just like riding in normal traffic with cars around you rather than having someone following you on a bike.' I nodded. 'I've parked the bike up so you can just ride it straight out of the car park easily. Don't forget to indicate as you go out of the car park. When you're doing your U turn remember to start turning when you look back and don't put your foot down. If you lose the examiner just pull over somewhere safe, though they usually tell you to do this anyway if they lose sight of you. Remember ...' As he rambled on through the endless reminders and tips he sounded determined to make sure I knew everything. I felt like I was being coached for a World Cup match or something. I was touched that he seemed to be almost trying to will me to pass, though unsure that I merited such faith. I looked at him and said 'Mark you need to prepare yourself for me to fail, okay?' He looked at me and said 'No, you're not going to fail, just do all the things we've taught you to do'. I had to laugh. 'Oh yes, just that, those few things you taught me to do, yeh right, easy then'. Mark grinned then asked me if I wanted him to get me a drink for when I got back. We agreed on coke and then I asked him 'If I do something that is obviously a fail, like put my foot down on the U turn, do I just pack in and head back?'. As the room was beginning to fill up with other candidates going out at the same time Mark whispered to me 'No. You carry on and do your very best on everything and then if you fail we can see the things you failed on and get them right for next time. Got that?' I nodded. We sat quietly for a minute then Mark whispered 'You might pass first time'. I turned to him and said 'Oh shut up'. He looked puzzled and bit hurt. Then he whispered 'I said, did Mike pass first time?' and I realised I had misheard him. 'No, he passed second time. Sorry for telling you to shut up I thought you said you might pass first time' I explained. 'Well you might' he whispered and then grinned at me.

Then my examiner came in, called out my name and took me into a side room to check my papers. He explained slowly and clearly exactly what was going to happen and helped me attach a mic to my jacket. He seemed at pains to be friendly and to help me relax. Even so there wasn't much chance of that happening. We headed out into the car park where he made me read out a car number plate and then he stood by the bike and said 'Is this your bike?' I said 'No, it belongs to the bike school'. He took down some details and then said ' A Kawasaki ER 500, do you like it?' What a strange question. 'No' I replied. He looked surprised. 'I usually ride a little cruiser, I prefer them' I said. He smiled and nodded. What did that mean? Is he a cruiser fan too? Will that put me in his good books? Then he got into his car, we tested that the mic was working and he told me to set off and take a left hand turn at the exit to the car park. As I let out the clutch and rolled forward my whole world seemed to shrink to just my head and the examiners voice in my helmet. I was so tense and nervous and trying so hard to concentrate that I cannot remember much about the first five minutes. Things only started to loosen up when having missed a lifesaver at one junction, I then stalled at the entrance to a roundabout so missed my chance to go. I then hesitated too long once I had got the bike started again because my nerves got the better of me. 'Poor observation and undue hesitation' I said to myself 'You idiot, you've failed'. Then I thought about what Mark had said and decided to just get through the rest of the test as best I could so I would only have to improve on the things I failed on. I began to relax. No point worrying when it was all over anyway. As I rode along I kept hearing Danny, Ian and Marks voices in my head. 'A life saver would be nice Jackie' and 'Look up at the junction for the speed limit' and 'Be nosy, look into the side streets at junctions'. On the U turn I could hear Mark saying 'Look back and start the turn' and Danny saying 'Foot downs a fail Jackie' so I looked then turned and willed my foot to stay on the peg and got round fine. I was so chuffed thinking 'I hope that wasn't a fail, I can't wait to see Mark's face'. As I pushed the bike across the road I could hear Mark saying 'Get it on full lock'. My emergency stop was okay which was amazing and as we headed into a country lane I could hear Ian saying 'Get up to speed Jackie but be safe'. Before I knew it I was being asked to ride back into the test centre car park. It all seemed to be over in minutes. As I rode in I looked around for Mark so that I could shake my head at him to let him see that I had failed but he was nowhere to be seen. I parked up and the examiner told me to go back to the little side room so that he could ask me some questions. I made my way to the room. Still no sign of Mark, where was he? The examiner came in and asked me to remove the mic, which I did and then he asked me all about carrying pillion passengers and I managed to answer those questions, all the time thinking why is he going through this charade, when any minute now he is going to fail me. So imagine my surprise when he said 'Well, you'll be pleased to hear that you've passed your test and …' He continued talking but I couldn't hear him. I think the combined effect of shock and disbelief and delight was affecting my hearing. I just stared at him. Then in the corner of my eye I saw Mark appear in the doorway of the waiting room opposite with a big grin on his face and both his thumbs stuck up in the air. He had been hiding round the corner and listening! I just looked at him, too stunned to respond. The examiner then quizzed me about one or two things that I had obviously done wrong but I had to apologise and say I couldn't remember. I was in a daze. He then filled out some forms, gave me some booklets, shook my hand, said 'Well done and take care' and left me standing there like I had been struck by lightening. I wandered over to the waiting room where Mark was standing. I started to shake and said 'I can't believe it, I just can't believe it'. Then Mark, who also looked a bit stunned, put his arms around me and gave me a big hug and said 'Well done.' I just stood there shaking my head in disbelief. Then Mark said 'You were very lucky because it sounded like you indicated incorrectly on a roundabout. That would usually be a fail'. I turned to look at him as he puzzled over this and then said 'Mark, shut up. The examiner obviously liked me so he decided to let me pass.' Mark snorted and shook his head as if to say 'What is she like?' and then we headed back out to the bikes. I borrowed

Mark's mobile phone to ring Mike, under strict instructions not
to natter on because his battery was low. When Mike answered I
yelled excitedly into the phone 'I've passed, yippee. It's all over
and I passed, ha, ha!' Mark looked embarrassed but I didn't care
because at last I was beginning to relax and enjoy this wonderful
moment. 'Oh well done' said Mike, sounding surprised and
delighted, 'does this mean you'll start sleeping with me again?' I
burst out laughing. 'Yes, of course it does but I can't talk because
Mark's battery is running out so see you soon' I called excitedly.
'Yes, okay, ride safely – well done' Mike sounded really chuffed
and I felt so proud. I handed Mark back his phone and gave him
a huge grin. He looked at me like I was slightly deranged, which
in fairness I probably was. I then drank the bottle of coke he had
been to buy me and we got ready to ride home. I was still shaking
a bit so had to wait a minute till I calmed down. Then we set off
back and I thought to myself how strange it was that I would now
be able to go out on a bigger bike on my own, with no L plates
and no instructor. I had started the day as a learner and was now
an approved big biker. It was amazing. I felt on top of the world,
anyone would think I had just flown to the moon and back or
discovered a cure for cancer I was so excited and proud of myself.
Riding home was weird. I kept laughing inside my helmet and
had to tell myself to concentrate. Mark was leading and suddenly
I noticed that his rucksack was sliding off the pillion seat. All
my paperwork was in there and I began to think that any minute
now it was going to fall off and I would ride right over it. I kept
watching it in case I had to do a real emergency stop but although
it was hanging over the side it stuck there. That took my mind off
passing my test for a while.

Back at the bike school everyone was very complementary but

it was obviously just another pass in a long line of passes that they saw every week so no cheering and champagne. Pity. I still felt a bit dazed. I said my goodbyes and drove home. Mike was waiting for me and as I walked into the house he rushed up and gave me a massive hug and said 'Well done mate, it's fantastic that you passed and first time too'. He was grinning and hugging and kissing me. Now this was more like it. The rest of the day was spent dancing round the house, laughing and giggling, ringing friends and relatives, especially mum to thank her for the spell and then rushing out to the garage to rip the L plates off my little Virago. Mike came to see what I was doing. 'I don't know why you're bothering with that, you'll be getting rid of it now and getting something bigger' he said, looking excited. I thought about this for a minute and said 'Yes, I suppose I will. I can now get the bigger one, the 535, but that isn't going to happen immediately and in any case, my little cruiser looks bigger than a 125 so if I take off the L plates people might think I'm riding a bigger bike.' Mike looked puzzled and then asked me 'What's the point of that?' 'Well, with no L plates on people will see that I am a fully qualified biker' I retorted feeling full of myself. 'Yes and then they'll think, why is that fully qualified biker being such a twit and riding so slow?' I hadn't thought of that. Yes I was going to have to get a bigger bike sorted out.

That evening I went out with everyone from work. I work part time at the local university. I used to work there full time but then left to concentrate on mine and Mike's business, but I still do it because I love the work and it is nice to get out of the house one day a week. It was Anne's leaving doo, in fact, and when she and Norman turned up the first thing she said was 'How did you get on?' I grinned and said 'I passed!' Anne's face broke into a huge smile. 'We knew you would, didn't we Norman? Norman said to me when you left our house the other week, she looks right confident on that bike, she'll be fine on her test'. Norman came over and hugged me and we talked about what had happened and I thanked them for their card. I told Anne it had made me cry and she said 'You daft bat, what are you like?' and we all burst out laughing. Then we all went bowling, where I did very well considering how tired my arms were. This was followed by a nice meal in a local Indian restaurant. With ten of us in the group, all bringing drinks with us, the booze was soon flowing and apart from one or two people who were driving, the rest of us were getting merrily sloshed. I couldn't stop talking about motorbikes and my test. My boss at the end of the table said, in his thick Scottish accent, 'What is she going on about?' and my colleague Alexa, also Scottish, said 'Oh ignore her, she won't stop talking about bloody motorbikes'. My boss works on a different campus so wasn't aware of my latest interest. 'What, she's neh into motorbikes now is she?' he said. I was about to respond and fill him in on all the details when Alexa, empty wine bottle in front of her, called out 'Aye, she's got one of those Yamaha Viagras'. Everyone stopped talking and looked up. 'A Yamaha Viagra, what the bloody hell is one of those?' asked my boss. 'It's a hot rod' said my colleague Bob who was sitting opposite and enjoying this conversation enormously. Everyone started to guffaw with laughter. 'It's not a Viagra, it's a Virago' I tried to explain but no one was listening. They were all playing around with the idea of a motorbike called a Viagra. Comments like 'goes like a rocket' and 'won't go round bends' and 'best bike for a hard ride' could be heard all round the table. From there on I can't remember much else about the evening. The next morning, suffering from a huge hangover, I told Mike what they had all said. He snorted with laughter. 'Viagra? Hardly, if you're thinking about your bike and sex I can think of another V word which would be far more appropriate'. I decided not to pursue that topic and just concentrate on finding some paracetamol.

Bike for sale

Whether you like it or not, you're going to have to sell in order to be successful. Learn to love it, and you'll achieve your goals far faster.
Geoffrey James

Later that morning, as my hangover began to subside, I decided to photograph my bike and then make up an advert to put up on the wall at the bike school. I had seen a few adverts up there and my little bike was so lovely that somebody doing their Compulsory Basic Training was sure to see it and want it. So I got the bike out and gave it a really good clean. I used to think that people who spent a lot of time cleaning their motorbikes were very sad and should get a life but I do exactly the same now. Bikes are not like cars, they cannot just be run through the car wash once a week. They need to be cleaned down carefully, every exposed part wiped clean and lovingly polished by hand so that they gleam.

All that chrome looks just beautiful when it is glistening in the sunshine. Some motorbikes look like they have, in the words of Annie Proux, been 'ridden hard and put away dirty' and I hate to see that. Besides which my bike is designed to be cleaned and shown off, it is not one of the drudges of the bike world so I have to get my chrome polish out like the rest of those sad people who spend part of their weekends making their machines look as good as new. With every bit of chrome gleaming and the rest of the paintwork buffed to sparkling perfection, I wheeled the bike onto the drive and photographed it from several angles. Then I put it back in the garage saying 'Sorry mate, you thought you were going out then didn't you, all clean and shiny but not just at the moment. I've got a bit of a hangover and it is not a good idea to ride in this state, so maybe later or tomorrow. Okay?' I don't know why I do that, talk to the bike, but I do. I decided not to mention the selling thing during our little chat, because I didn't want any trouble from the bike whilst it was still mine. Then I downloaded the picture onto my computer and put together an advert which read:

For Sale
Yamaha Virago 125cc
One year old, one careful lady owner from new, 2,000 dry miles, full service history, taxed for 12 months, datatagged, immaculate condition. £1,850 Telephone Jackie or Mike on …

'There, that ought to attract the punters' I thought. Then I looked at the picture of my lovely little bike and felt a twinge of guilt. How could I sell it? I felt like a traitor. If only I had enough money and a huge garage, I would keep it and buy a bigger one. But I didn't have enough money and the garage was only really big enough for two motorbikes, two pushbikes and all the gardening tools, so it was not to be. I printed out a couple of copies of my home made advert and then, calling in at the local newsagents to buy a box of Thank You chocolates, I rode up to the school to stick it on the wall in the office where all the learners check in for their training. Ian and Danny were in the office so I handed over the chocolates and said 'These are to say thank you. Did Mark tell you?' Ian looked a bit puzzled and said 'Tell me what?' I couldn't help but grin, 'I passed, yesterday'. Danny then piped up 'Well, that's because of that first lesson you had with me. I obviously got you off to a flying start'. Ian rolled his eyes upwards. 'Well, actually Mark thought I was lucky to pass, because I think I did something wrong on a roundabout' I said. At this point Mark, who had been sitting round the corner in the restroom, appeared in the doorway and started to describe what I had done wrong. Ian interrupted him and asked me how many faults were recorded on my Driving test report sheet. I fished the sheet out of my bag and looked at it. There were a total of four driving faults, all of them minor. Ian looked at the form, read off the examiner's name and said 'Well you must have ridden well overall because this bloke is a strict examiner and to only get four minors is really good'. I felt lightheaded with pride. I looked at Mark and so wanted to stick my tongue out at him and go 'Nar, nar, na, nar, nar' but managed to resist the urge. Ian looked pleased, both for me and I suppose because my passing was another success for their school. I asked if I could stick my advert on the wall and they readily agreed but then Danny said to me 'You ought to sell it on eBay, you know?' Danny explained that he had sold a couple of motorbikes that way, so I decided to take a look at it to see if that was an option too.

The following day I had a good look at eBay and was amazed at how many motorbikes were for sale on it. Reading some of the adverts I realised that using eBay would give me a lot more scope to describe my motorbike in detail but I would also have to be honest and explain any problems or faults too. It looked like a good way to sell the bike so I spent the rest of the afternoon composing a long description that I could submit. It read:

Yamaha 125cc cruiser

Year of reg: 2002

Mileage: 3,500 km (2,200 miles)

I bought this bike last year after doing my CBT course and I love it. I have kept it in immaculate condition; it is datatagged and kept in a garage when I am not riding it in the sunshine in the Derbyshire Dales. I have done 2,200 dry miles on it (3,500 kilometres on the clock). It runs superbly. I went to Leeds on it not long ago and the petrol for the 200 mile return journey cost £6.00. Top speed on the flat about 60mph. Full service history, tax for 12 months and I have never had a problem with it at all. I will be sorry to sell it but having now passed my Direct Access course (mainly due to all the practice on this lovely machine) I want to buy her bigger sister, the 535, so I can keep up with my husband. The buyer must collect from Stafford and pay cash on collection or send a personal cheque and the bike will be handed over when the cheque clears. If you would like to view the bike before bidding please contact me on (my mobile number) or email me. Please only bid if you intend to buy. The bike is advertised elsewhere so I reserve the right to withdraw it from eBay.

So with my blurb now written I then set about trying to work out how to put it on eBay. Well, call me stupid if you like, but I could not work it out, or how much it would cost or how you got people to pay. So I decided to email them to ask for help. They promptly replied, providing me with links to the web pages that I had already been reading all evening and could not make much sense of. Talk about going round in circles. So I gave up and went to bed feeling defeated and technically useless. Why is it that some people seem to be able to pick these things up so quickly? I use computers and the internet every day but I still find it very hard to get my head around some of this stuff. I decided to wait and see if my advert in the bike school attracted any buyers and resigned myself to continuing to ride my 125 for the foreseeable future.

The following week Jim turned up with a cheque to pay for Mike's bike. His wife came along with him. I think she wanted to get a look at us before they handed over a big cheque to relative strangers. The arrangement was that Mike would ring Jim when the cheque had cleared so that Jim could then call round and collect the bike. Very trusting when you think about it. We had a long chat about bikes and I tried not to boast too much about passing my test. My glory was undermined a bit by Mike saying 'Well, she might have passed her bike test first time but it took her three goes to pass her driving test in the car'. I just looked at him. What had that got to do with anything? That was over 20 years ago. He then went on to say 'It took me two goes to pass my bike test but I passed my driving test first time, so it's swings and roundabouts really'. What was he on about? I decided to stay quiet and quiz him later. Then Jim's wife and I ended up talking about Yorkshire and how and why we had ended up living in the Midlands, because it turned out she was originally from Bradford. I asked her if she was going to learn to ride and she laughed. 'No way. And I've told Jim I'm not going on the back of his either. The only bike you would get me on the back of is a Harley Davidson. Now if he buys one of those I would go out with him' she said, a wistful look in her eye. Mike's face lit up. He had been in touch with the Harley garage and booked a test ride on a V Rod, much to my dismay, and now seemed delighted to have a pro Harley visitor. 'Yes, they're nice aren't they?' he said looking at Jim's wife and then me. He obviously thought that I would be swayed by hearing another Yorkshire lass singing the Harleys praises. 'What is it about these Harley Davidson's' I said 'everyone is mad about them'. At this point Jim piped up and said 'Oh I don't know about that. A friend of ours had one and every time he went out on it something fell off it.' I looked at him. 'What?' He continued. 'Yes, when he used to go out with a group of the lads, you know on a ride out, they always made sure someone rode behind him so they could stop and pick up the bits and then they'd give them back to him when they stopped.' I started to laugh and turned towards Mike to see what his response to this illuminating statement was going to be. Mike was grinning too but said 'Yes, they did used to be a bit clunky and agricultural but the new ones are much better. The new V Rod is supposed to be superb.' He gave me a knowing look but Jim then chimed in with 'That's that new one isn't it, that really expensive, flash one?' Mike nodded so Jim continued 'Yes, it's not a proper Harley though, that one, is it? It's too modern and too flash.' Mike mumbled something about that being no bad thing if bits don't fall off it and then, because Jim and his wife had to be somewhere else soon, the conversation switched to final arrangements for collecting the Honda. As we said our goodbyes it suddenly struck me that Mike was soon going to be without a bike.

A couple of days later, whilst eating tea, it suddenly occurred to me that Mike should have had his test ride on the V Rod. I asked him when it was booked, thinking I must have got my dates mixed up. I was right though, he should have gone that day but he had rung up and cancelled. 'Why did you cancel?' I asked. 'Well, the weather was a bit rotten and I didn't really fancy going out on a strange bike and in any case they are ridiculously expensive and I'm not sure I can see the point in test riding one if I am not going to seriously consider buying one'. I had to stop myself from grinning. My tactics of saying nothing had obviously paid off! Left to his own devices and with nothing (and no one) to push against he had obviously come to his senses. I just managed to stop myself yelling 'YES!' and punching the air with my fist. Instead I kept my face straight and serious and said 'Okay, so what other bikes do you fancy?' He looked down at his plate and said 'Well I've been thinking about getting a muscle bike, you know, like Alex's over the road'. That sounded a bit ominous. 'A muscle bike? What's a muscle bike?' I asked. 'It's one with a much bigger engine, you know something like 1200cc' he replied nonchalantly as he tucked into his meal. I almost choked on my dinner. '1200cc! Are you mad? That's a car on two wheels. What do you want one of them for?' I spluttered. Mike looked a bit taken aback at my shocked response as he is usually quite good at predicting how I am going to react to things and he obviously wasn't expecting me to baulk like this. He looked at me warily and then said 'What's the matter with 1200ccs? There's no point me getting anything much smaller because it'll be the same as riding the Honda. Anyway, you've seen Alex's. It is just another motorbike.' Just another motorbike. Was he blind? Alex's 1200 Suzuki Bandit was a mechanical monster that roared away from the house like a jet fighter taking off. Now that I thought about it I remembered that Alex had once pointed out to us that you have to open the throttle on these bikes really carefully if you don't want the front end to rear up, unless you want to do wheelies of course. So, just another motorbike. I was horrified and was about to launch into a hysterical rant against muscle bikes when I suddenly remembered that the way to success in these matters was to stay quiet. That approach had produced good results in the V Rod debacle so perhaps I should stick with this approach as it was proving to be a winning strategy. So, instead of ranting, I took a deep breath, nodded my head and tried to look as if I was giving this new idea some serious thought and then said 'Well, okay, if that's what you want, perhaps we should go look at some'. Mike looked at me suspiciously and I realised I needed to be more careful. Such sudden U turns on my part were sure to make him suspicious and I didn't want him working out what was going on. I decided to change the subject, quickly. 'Have you ever tried to use that ebay auction site? Danny suggested I sell my bike on it but I can't get to grips with it. Do you know how to use it?' I asked him, knowing that the other subject bound to catch his attention was anything to do with computers. 'No, but I know loads of people use it. I don't know why you're bothering with that though. You should get it advertised in the bike magazine, that's where everyone looks for bikes.' We talked it through a bit and I decided he might be right so I made a mental note to go and buy a copy the next day to see what you had to do to get your bike sold.

The following week Jim's cheque cleared and his mate turned up to collect the bike. I can't say I was sorry to see it go because I never had been that fond of it but it left us in a sorry state on the motorbike front. Me now eligible to ride a big bike but still with my little 125, and Mike with no bike at all. It was not good, we had to get things sorted out.

Muscle bikes

Muscle bike is a nickname for a motorcycle type, derived from either a standard or sport bike design, that puts a disproportionately high priority on engine power.
Types of motorcyles – Wikipedia

Putting an advert in the biking magazine was simplicity itself after the technological challenges of eBay. Using the same wording from my little advert at the bike school, I cut the form out of the magazine, filled it in and posted it off with my cheque. Easy. The next edition was due out the following month so I decided to concentrate my energies on getting Mike to find and buy a new bike. He seemed to be having trouble drumming up enthusiasm for the task and I began to worry that he was going to lose interest in the whole thing and not bother getting another bike. So at the weekend I dragged him off to the bike showroom where I had bought my little cruiser. Whilst he wandered around near the big machines I went looking for Virago 535's. I found two. One was a lovely blue colour but looked like it had put in a few hard miles with an owner who wasn't too worried about keeping it clean and scratch free. The other was pristine but a sort of muddy fudge and brown colour that did nothing for me. I got chatting to a salesman who came over, called Chris and told him I had bought my 125 from them and, just out of interest, what would they give me for it in part exchange if I decided to buy one of these 535's? I thought I had misheard him when he quoted me a figure that was just over half the price I had paid for the bike only one year earlier. 'How much?' I gasped, really meaning to say 'How little?' I couldn't believe it. He went on to explain that there wasn't a massive market for these bikes and the price of the new ones had fallen and they had to give warranties with them and so on and so forth. He ended by saying 'You'd be better off selling it privately, you'll get more for it that way'. I couldn't have agreed more and standing there listening to him I resolved to do just that. Yes, one way or another I was going to sell my bike privately and not only that, I was also going to buy my next one privately because obviously buying from a dealer meant you were going to pay top whack. The salesman must have sensed my interest was cooling because he said 'Look, if you like the look of this one you can always take it out for a test ride. All we need is your driving licence and passport and you have to sign a form accepting responsibility for the first £500's worth of damage.' I said I would think about it and then wandered over to join Mike who was looking over a Suzuki GSX1400 and I could instantly see why these machines are called muscle bikes. This one looked like it had been on steroids and working out at the gym. The engine was bulging out from where it was crammed in under the seat, it made me think of the incredible hulk just before his clothes all rip and split. I just stood and stared in disbelief. Then I heard Mike laughing and saying to me 'What?' Working hard to stick to my non-confrontational strategy I replied 'Nothing. It's big isn't it, the engine I mean, it's spilling out of the bike'. Mike just laughed again. The salesman, who had followed me across the showroom, started to sing the bike's praises to Mike and they were soon lost in a technical conversation about bhps and torque. I stood idly by, trying to act nonchalant until I heard the phrase 'the speedo goes up to 180'. The words were out before I could stop them. '180 miles an hour? That's ridiculous. When are you ever going to go that fast?' The salesman looked at me with a gleam in his eye and said 'Well that's just letting you know that it can go that fast if you want it to' and then seeing the look of horror on my face he quickly added 'but obviously you wouldn't go that fast, that's totally illegal'. Mike just looked at me, grinned and shrugged his shoulders as if to say 'it's just one of those things you wouldn't understand'. Ooh men, what is it with them and fast machines and speed? I was beginning to think that bringing Mike here was a big mistake but then when I looked at him closely I could tell that he wasn't that enamoured with this mountain of metal. 'So you're interested in a bigger bike, well we've got a nice Honda Hornet CB900 over here, come and listen to this' said Chris, as he led Mike up the row to another bike. This one wasn't quite so muscle bound and looked quite trim in comparison to the Suzuki. The saleman said 'Just let me get the keys'. He was back in a flash and after manoeuvring the bike out into the aisle he started it up. Over the roar of the engine he yelled 'Listen to that. One of the greatest assets in a salesman's armoury, the sweet sound of a good engine. Just listen to that' and he revved it up 'lovely isn't it?' I listened but I wouldn't say it sounded lovely. It sounded like a motorbike to me. Maybe motorbike engine noises are like wine, it takes time to appreciate the finer ones. Mike was smiling but I could tell he wasn't that taken with this bike either. The yellow paintwork, with lots of bright zigzags and streaks, didn't help much. This bike looked like it should be zooming round a race track, not gently cruising through the countryside of the Derbyshire Dales. After a bit more technical tittle tattle we decided to call it a day and headed off home.

On the way back we talked about the two bikes we'd seen. 'They were okay but they didn't interest me that much. I preferred the Honda but I've just sold a CB500 which was similar so I'm not sure I want to fork out for a bike that is only just a bit bigger than what I've already had,' said Mike. I was starting to get worried. Mike has a habit of picking up and dropping new interests and I didn't want to end up in the position he had been in, in other words, with a motorbike but without someone to come out on rides with me. 'Look, let's call in at the Honda dealers and see what else they've got because you do seem to like Hondas' I suggested. 'Okay' said Mike sounding bored and tired. Once inside he perked up a bit and started to look over a Honda CB1300. This was another contender for the Arnold Schwarzenegger look-alike competition. Big, bulging and very, very heavy. I noticed later it was described in a magazine as 'Stonking motor meets sure footed handling in a mountain of metal'. See what I mean? It only seemed to come in two colour schemes; red and white which made it look like a big mechanical mascot for a football team, and black which made it look like something that Darth Vadar might ride. These bikes are not pretty. Mike asked if he could test ride it but they said they didn't offer test rides at this dealership. He didn't look that disappointed. Now

I was getting really worried. What was the matter with him? He didn't seem interested in any bikes. That night, whilst watching TV, I decided to try and find out why he was so apathetic about the whole thing. 'So, which bike do you think you might go for?' I asked, using my casual 'do you want a cup of tea then' voice. Mike glanced up at me with a 'Don't know' expression on his face. It was the sort of look that teenagers have on their faces when they mumble 'Whatever'. This was worrying. 'Did you like the CB1300 that we saw today?' I asked. 'Not really' he said sounding bored. I could see this was going be one of those pulling teeth conversations. 'Why not?' He thought for a moment then said 'Well, I didn't much like the look of it and the colour schemes don't do anything for me.' Oh dear. As an arts graduate Mike is always quite concerned with how things look visually so this was not some little thing that wouldn't really count in the overall assessment of any motorbike. This was a big sticking point. I wasn't sure how to proceed. 'So you want a bike that looks nice. So which bikes do you think are nice looking then?' It took me about two seconds to realise that this was not the thing to ask and as my mind leapt into action my mouth opened and out popped the words 'The V Rod'. I don't know why I do that. Just blurt out the words that pop into my mouth. Mike looked at me in a way that was either uncertain or calculating, I couldn't decide, and I began to wonder if he too was playing a tactical game. His game might be something like 'sell the bike, show no interest in any other bike, wife begins to worry that she won't have a biking partner, wife gives in to purchase of V Rod'. I sat and mulled this over. Could this be his game plan? It was hard to decide because in my experience men aren't that devious, it's we women that play these sorts of mind games. Men usually just don't get them so they either just say what they think or say nothing at all. So which was it? I decided to wait it out and see what he said next. Mike acted like he was mulling this suggestion over and then said 'Well, yes, all the critics say the new V Rod is stunning looking but we've already agreed that they cost too much so that's out. I just need to keep looking.' I mulled this over. If he was playing mind games this was a good move. He was still letting me know he was interested in the V Rod but then stepping back from it because he knew I was struggling to accept the cost of one. Very good move. I decided to leave things alone and let him keep looking. He might find something that would be equally appealing. Who was I kidding?

Over the next few days I noticed him reading lots of biking magazines and reviews of different bikes but it always seemed to be the V Rod articles that were left lying around the longest. One magazine in particular had a fantastic picture of a V Rod on the front as it posed at the Cannes Film Festival. Inside the writer enthused about the bike and said that riding it was a bit like flying a hover bike from the Star Wars film The Return of the Jedi. I had to admit to myself that it did look fantastic and sounded like a lot of fun. Also I couldn't help liking it because it's a cruiser, which is my preferred kind of motorbike anyway. After several days of Mike moping around the house and a glorious weekend when I had to go out on the Virago on my own, I finally caved in. 'Oh why don't you book another test ride on a V Rod. Let's go and see what all the fuss is about.' We were in the office and the sun was shining outside and, as I sat at my computer, I just thought 'Oh what the hell. Maybe if he test rides one he won't like it anyway. He has never been that keen on cruisers.' Mike didn't say anything, probably realising that his 'You've changed your tune' catch phrase might lose him this window of opportunity to try out the one bike that had really grabbed his interest. So he rang the garage and booked a ride.

The V Rod

It is interesting to watch a Harley showroom on a weekend day. Men come in and three feet inside the door they stop and a kind of stunned, glazed look comes into their eyes as they walk around and touch the bikes, just touch them, and dream and hope and wish.
Zero to Sixty: The motorcycle journey of a lifetime. Gary Paulsen.

Over the intervening days Mike cheered up enormously and I began to think that maybe he was playing a tactical game and was feeling proud of himself for winning this latest move. I said nothing because I couldn't work out what my next move should be. Also, I have to admit that I too was curious about this new wonder bike that everyone was raving about and wanted to get a closer look at it. On the morning of his test ride the weather was very changeable, one minute bright sunshine and the next overcast and cloudy. It looked like it might rain. Mike looked out of the bedroom window and said 'Maybe I should cancel the ride and wait for a better day'. I couldn't believe it. My bike was due to appear in the Bike Trader magazine any day now and would hopefully sell. I would then get a bigger bike and we would take to the road as a couple of big bikers. Well that was my plan and here he was still without a bike and doing nothing to get one. This was not going to happen. 'Look, today is as good as any so just get on with it' I snapped as I stumbled out of bed. Whilst he made breakfast I stood in the shower and wondered how we had got to the situation where I was the one pushing him to test ride a V Rod! Over breakfast he asked me if I was going to go with him to see the bike. It crossed my mind to say no and show no interest as a way of signaling my disapproval but I wanted to see this bike. Curiosity doesn't only kill cats, it loses you the high ground in marital arguments. 'Yes, of course, I am coming to see the bike' I said. He smiled and nodded but I noticed that he looked a bit troubled about something. 'What is it? What's the matter? Are you worrying about taking this bike out?' I asked. 'No, it's not that, it's just, well, I don't know my way around that area. I just hope I can remember the route.' We had looked at a map the night before and worked out a route which took him out of the town and round the countryside a bit and then back into the town but from a different direction. As biking doesn't really lend itself to map reading and Mike usually writes down his route and keeps referring to his list of directions as he drives along, this could pose a problem. Mike is hopeless at remembering routes and not too good at following road signs though he denies this vigorously when challenged. I could see straight away that this might be a problem. Then I had an idea. 'I tell you what, why don't I ride over on my bike and come round on the ride with you. That gives me a good excuse to get the bike out and between us we should be able to find our way back okay.' His face lit up with a big smile and I knew then that he didn't want to do this on his own. It felt nice knowing that my best mate wanted me to help him with this mini adventure.

So he put his gear in the car and I got the bike out and rode over to the Harley garage. As I pulled into the car park and parked up next to a long row of Harley Davidson cruisers I felt really excited. My little Virago looked like a David standing next to a line of Goliaths. Mike pulled in shortly afterwards. 'You made good time, I kept thinking I would pass you on route but I obviously never caught up with you' he said as we walked into the showroom. I looked at him and smiled. He never has accepted that I can go quite fast on my little cruiser. We went in and sorted out all the paperwork you have to fill in to get a test ride and then came out to look at the bike he was going to ride. The paintwork was silver with a sort of purple licking flames paint job. Very fancy. I thought to myself "If this bike were a person it would be a sort of cross between Arni as The Terminator and Elvis at his very sexy best in one of his white leather, 'look at me, I'm a sex machine' outfits". After a 2 minute tour of the controls and a 5 minute lesson from the salesman on how to work the bike alarm system, we got our gear on and set off. I noticed there were a few smiles as I led the V Rod out of the compound on my tiny cruiser. I felt like a tug boat leading out an ocean liner. As we pulled around the corner from the showroom we rode straight into a traffic jam. Great. We sat and waited. Then waited some more. My bike got hotter and hotter. What was going on? I tried to pull out and see ahead and then realised that there had been some sort of crash on the road ahead and there were police cars and ambulances and, well, no one was going anywhere on that road. Just what we needed. I signalled to Mike to pull up near to me and yelled over the throb of the engines what was going on. We decided to try and turn the bikes and go the other way. This was not too bad for me as I was used to zipping around on my little bike but was quite a challenge for Mike. The V Rod might be described as long and lean but trying to manhandle a nearly six foot long, 600lb arrangement of metal, especially when you have never ridden it before and you have an audience of bored drivers with nothing else to watch, can be hard work. After much huffing and puffing and a 49 point turn we eventually managed to set off in the other direction, all our planned routes for the test ride now out of the window. I was leading so I began to think frantically about where we were and how to get back on track. Years before I had done a night class for two years in this town so I vaguely remembered some of the road system. I led us off in a different direction and headed out of town following a slightly different route. Gradually we worked our way back to the original road of our plans. It was hard work trying to follow the road signs and work out the route whilst constantly checking my rear mirrors to see that Mike was still following me. I knew that if I lost him he would be hopeless at finding his way back and would probably spend the rest of the day riding around in the sprawling, interlocking conurbations that are the Black Country (pronounced Blek Cun-tray). Finally we were out on the open road so I waited for Mike to overtake me so he could experience that effortless, low down power that everyone was raving about, but he just stayed tucked in behind me. I began to think that maybe all that 'freefall' navigating had unnerved him so he now felt very unsure about our route so he was going to stick to following me. What a pity, the whole point of a test ride is to get the feel for what a bike can do. I decided to try and go faster so he could go faster so I opened up the throttle and wound the bike up to about 55 miles an hour. Fortunately we were on a flat, open road so my little cruiser could just about manage this but as soon as we began to tackle an incline my bike lost speed. This was ridiculous. Eventually I pulled over into a lay-by and waited for him to pull up behind me. He lifted up his visor, a big grin on his face and asked 'What's the matter?' 'Nothing's the matter, but aren't you going to overtake me, you'll never get a feel for the bike if you stick behind me' I said. What was I thinking? I had completely forgotten about the fact that I didn't want him to like this bike and instead was getting caught up in the moment and wanting to see what this bike could really do. As I suspected Mike was feeling very unsure about the route so we agreed that he would lead the rest of the way on the country roads but as soon as we rode back inside the city lines I would move to the front. I then remembered I had my camera with me so I took a picture of him sitting on the bike. I had planned to use this to console him by saying 'Look you may not own one but you can show people that you have ridden one'. He loved that picture. He had it in his office and he emailed it as an attachment to anyone we knew that was interested in bikes. He even emailed it to an old girlfriend who contacted him via Friends Reunited, which I thought was hilarious as he is wearing his crash helmet in the picture so you can hardly see his face. You see, Harleys and posing go hand in hand!

For the next part of the ride he did begin to pull away from me and I have to admit he looked good sitting astride this state of the art cruiser. When it's moving the bike has a certain grace and poise and it reminded me of when I used to watch Torvill and Dean, the ice skaters. They would swoop around the rink at high speed but always in a smooth and graceful way and the V

Rod is like that. It glides along the road. Also, it's very quiet for a Harley, with a sort of low down rumble rather than the usual loud 'bum bum bum' noise that our neighbour says sounds like someone saying 'potato, potato' in a very low and gruff voice. I couldn't help it, I was beginning to really like the look of this bike and I wasn't the only one. As we rode back into the city we joined a very slow moving line of traffic that eventually turned into a creeping traffic jam around a set of road works. Funneled into one narrow lane by traffic cones, there was nothing we could do but crawl along at a snail's pace. The coned off side of the road was full of lorries and workmen laying new tarmac. As we trundled past they started to look over at us and all eyes quickly focused on the V Rod. The men began calling to each other 'Oy, look at this bike here" and work stopped whilst everyone got a good look at it. One older man came over and started asking Mike about it. "Is that one of them new Harley's – that rod thing?' Obviously we were passing through one of those secret pockets of the biking world where everyone is a biker. More men started wandering over and asking questions. One bloke took pity on me and said 'I bet you wish you had one of those". I was about to say 'No, I love my little Virago' but managed to stop myself and agree, "Yes, in my dreams". It sounded like the right sort of thing to say in that situation. As the men huddled round the V Rod the traffic ahead pulled away and I rode on. I watched in my rear view mirror as Mike reluctantly pulled himself away from his new found fan club. When we pulled up again I looked over at him and, even with a helmet on, I could see he was grinning from ear to ear. As we pulled back onto the Harley garage forecourt I knew the battle was lost. He was in love with this bike and nothing else was going to come near it. We parked up and I walked over to him. He was still smiling. 'So, what did you think?' I asked. 'It was amazing, not at all like the Honda, it just pulls away in every gear. It's a completely different riding experience, it's amazing'. Now he was laughing too. Oh dear, what was I thinking when I encouraged him to go for a test ride? However, on the plus side he was once again showing a real interest in bikes even if it was the wrong bike. I decided to keep quiet and let this thing play out. The salesman came over and him and Mike spent about ten minutes enthusing about the bike, talking prices and delivery times. I left them to it and rode home. That evening I raised the subject again over tea. 'What did you say to the workmen, when they came over to look at the bike?' 'I just told them that, yes, it was the new Harley V rod'. Mr Nonchalant. 'They seemed quite impressed with it' I said. 'Yes, they were asking me what they cost.' 'So, did you tell them?' I asked, interested to hear what Mike had said. The one thing that puts people off these bikes is the cost. At that time, a new V Rod was around £14,000 and this usually made most people blanch. I wondered what he had said to them. 'I told them they were about 14 grand new.' 'And …?' I waited to hear more. 'And what?' he asked, between mouthfuls. 'What did they say to that…14 grand for a motorbike ..?' I was beginning to sound exasperated, which is not surprising when you consider how hard we women sometimes have to work to keep a conversation going with our dearly beloveds. 'Well, they thought it was a lot of money but I told them I was just test riding it and it wasn't mine'. Mike had a sort of 'Well obviously it wouldn't be mine at that sort of price' look on his face. This was going to be interesting. Clearly he wanted one but was having difficulty justifying the cost. Could I use this embarrassment to my advantage, I wondered. 'Well, they are a lot of money, aren't they?' As soon as I said this I knew it was the wrong thing to say. My 'Didn't I tell you, mum knows best' tone of voice sounded patronising even to me. 'Well maybe it is a lot of money but you only live once and that is one hell of a bike. In any case, it will probably hold it's value, I mean it's already a design icon.'

Oh no, not a design icon. He loves design icons. Furniture, no matter how uncomfortable, kitchen appliances, retro looking and needed about twice a year, Mike is drawn to design icons like a magnet to metal. He loves them. I knew then that he was never to going to settle for any other bike. Nothing was going to come near this machine and I could either fight him all the way and probably end up biking on my own or give up the struggle and work out how we were going to pay for one. I decided, in the interest of my own biking ambitions, to go for the latter and the rest of the evening was spent discussing new versus second hand, loans versus savings, and timescales. Oh well, you can't win 'em all.

Love at first ride

You won't have to tap on people's shoulders and tell them how cool you are, because a Harley will do it for you. Once you get a Harley, you don't even need a relationship. I want one so bad, my nipples sting just thinking about it.
Flaming Iguanas: An All-Girl Road Novel Thing, Erika Lopez

With my advert about to go in the Bike Trader magazine I realised that I needed to get on with my search for a new bike. My experience at the bike dealers where I had bought my Virago had left me determined to buy any new bike, second hand. I knew I would get a better deal that way. So I started trawling the Virago adverts on the bike trader website. There were quite a few and it was difficult to know where to start. In the end I decided to try and find one close enough to home to go and test ride it. I finally settled on one about fifty miles away. I rang the owner and arranged to go see it the following weekend. It was a lovely sunny

day when we set off and I was so excited. 'I can't believe I've
done it, I mean passed my test and all that, and now I'm going to
get a big bike'. At this last comment Mike snorted with laughter.
'Hardly a big bike, more like a tart's handbag if you ask me'.
'Well I'm not asking you. A 535 will be quite big enough for
me, thank you. The magazines might call it a tart's handbag
but in Nick Berry's book he said, and I quote, 'one of the best
motorcycles which anyone can start a two-wheeled career on',
so that's good enough for me.' Mike grinned but said nothing.
We arrived at the address and there, parked on the road, was a
Yamaha Virago 535. My heart sang. We parked up and went to
talk to the owner who was giving the bike a bit of a wipe down.
In fact, the bike was a bit grubby looking close up and the chrome
didn't sparkle like that on my little cruiser but I knew I could put
that right with a bit of tender, loving cleaning. We chatted about
the bike and it's history and looked it over and then the owner
offered to let me test ride it. So I put on my gear and headed out
on a circular route that the owner had described for me. I was
very nervous, it being a different bike for me to handle but once
I got the hang of it I settled down and tried to get a feel for the
bike and how it rode. The answer was, not very well. It felt lumpy
and unresponsive. Yes, it had more power when I opened the
throttle but it seemed to chug along reluctantly. It reminded me of
the Kawasaki I had trained on and not at all like my own lovely
cruiser back home. I felt my enthusiasm ebb away. This was not
the thrilling ride I had anticipated. I made my way back to the
house and pretended it was okay. The man encouraged Mike to
have a ride too, which was a mistake because I knew that nothing
that was going to happen out on the road was going to impress
Mike as to the merits of this particular bike. I waited and chatted
with the owner. It turned out he hadn't ridden the bike for ages,

it wasn't taxed and hadn't been serviced in over two years. He and his family wanted the money to pay for a holiday abroad and although he liked the bike he felt he had to put his family first. So, an unwanted bike with an indifferent owner, not good news. My immediate reaction was to think 'I can rescue this bike, love it, give it the home it deserves' but the ride had left me with several doubts as to whether the 535 would ever feel great. Mike came back and pretended he had also enjoyed himself but then he said we had others to see and we needed to think about it and we would get back to them after the weekend. I knew that translated this meant 'Forget it, we're out of here!'

The journey home was glum. I was very fed up. Mike's impression of the bike had echoed mine and to say he was unimpressed was something of an understatement. 'What on earth do you want one of those for, they're plodding donkeys. It handled like a milk crate on wheels. What on earth are you thinking of?' 'Oh shut up' I wailed. 'That can't have been a proper 535. It was nothing like mine. It wasn't even a cruising position. And in any case, what do you suggest I get?' I said. 'I don't know, but not one of them!' What a mess. Here we were, Mike without a bike, me with a 125 and all my dreams of us cruising off into the sunset together on two beautiful gleaming cruisers, well and truly scuppered. I mulled the situation over but couldn't shake off the idea that the right bike for me was my little Virago's bigger sister. I decided to go back to the big bike dealers and have another look at the ones they had. Mike drove me up there and I took everything I needed for a test ride. After a bit of discussion I arranged to take one of their 535's out on the road. This one had been cleaned, serviced and looked after and looked much better. So it was with a sinking heart that I quickly realised that the ride quality was no different. The bike definitely felt like it was plodding along. Mike didn't bother to test ride it, having already decided it was a non-starter. Once again, I returned home feeling glum.

A couple of days later the Harley garage rang to say they had a second hand V Rod that Mike might be interested in and did he want to come over and test ride it? We had decided that a brand new one was not really an option and so Mike was now on the look out for a good second hand one. Once again we decided that I would ride over and accompany him on the test ride. When we arrived at the dealership the salesman, who really looked the part with his big red beard, was stood in the yard having a smoke and he saw me ride in on the Virago. He came over and chatted to Mike and showed him the bike that was for sale. It stood gleaming in the sun, looking every inch the design icon it was. I stood and watched these two men as they circled the bike and discussed its various features. Mike was enthralled. Red, the salesman presumably named for his beard, was more circumspect saying he actually preferred the traditional Harleys but there was no getting away from the fact that the V Rod was in a class of it's own. On reflection, Red took exactly the right approach with Mike. He was honest in his appraisal of the bike and did not go for a really hard sell. This worked a treat. Mike is always suspicious of anyone trying it on with a hard sell, believing that if a thing is good it will sell itself and you don't need some over zealous salesperson trying to convince you of it's merits. This sort of 'You decide for yourself once you've ridden it" approach put Mike at ease. I do sometimes wonder 'How hard can it be to sell Harley's?' Saying this would probably infuriate all those men and women working hard in Harley showrooms up and down the country but these bikes are so beautiful and retro, the 'eye candy' of the biking world, guaranteed to make you feel like an 'oh so cool rebel' that how can anyone not want to buy one? Well, there is the small matter of the price, which is going to be a stumbling block for most punters but that's an issue of 'Can I afford it?' not 'Would I like to own one of these bikes?'. Having said that, I do know that there are bikers out there that hate Harleys with a vengence. They see them as outdated, underperforming, noisy old things which, in some ways they are, but there is just something about them which makes the rest of us love them. Then Red asked me what I thought of the V Rod. I agreed it was lovely and that it made my little cruiser look like a child's plaything. Jokingly, I said 'If he buys one of those things I am never going to be able to keep up with him', at which point the salesman said 'Well how big is that one?' pointing at the Virago. I told him it was a 125 and he was surprised and said he thought it was bigger than that. Then when I explained that I was going to accompany Mike on the ride he said something that, on reflection, changed everything. 'Why don't you test ride a Sportster at the same time? That way you can keep up with him." As he said this he turned and pointed to a lovely looking machine standing at the end of the line. 'That one there is a demonstrator, you could go out on that one. Have you got your licence with you?' Had I got my licence with me? Yes I had. It was still in my bike jacket pocket from when I had test ridden the Virago. My mind was racing. I could do this, I had my licence. I couldn't possibly do this, it was a Harley. It was too big. How big was it? No, Mike was the one who was having a Harley, not me. Why not me? I couldn't possibly ride a Harley? Why couldn't I ride a Harley? My legs turned to jelly and I just stood there with my mouth open. Mike then piped up. "What a great idea. Yes, you go on the Sportster.' The salesman had already started manoeuvring it out onto the yard. "It's an 883, which is a bit bigger than what you've got now but it's not a lot different to ride. It's not the cruiser position you're used to but that can be easily rectified. You would just get one with front pegs fitted.' Once he had the bike pulled out of line he looked over at me and, realising I was scared stiff, he invited me to sit on the bike to see how it felt. Now it was standing in front of me it didn't look so big. With it's peanut shaped petrol tank and slim V twin engine it actually looked quite sleek. I sat on it and then pulled it up off it's side stand. It felt heavy but it felt good. I started grinning, that sort of inane grinning you do when you are drunk, relaxed and happy. I don't know what it is about these motorbikes but they just make you feel good when you sit on them. They have what Mike's dad calls the 'WOW' factor. I tried to act nonchalant even though I was grinning like a Cheshire cat. 'So shall we get you set up to go out on that one then?' asked Red. 'Well, I don't know, I'm not used to…' 'You'll be fine. Right, give me your licence, let's get you sorted' and ten minutes later I found myself sitting on a Harley Davidson Sportster Roadster 883, fully kitted up and ready to ride. I felt like I was in a dream. Mike was manoeuvering the V Rod towards the gates and I was lined up facing them, waiting to go. 'Off you go then, see you later' said the salesman, turning to join a few other members of staff who had come out to watch. My mouth was dry. My internal voice began the pep talk. 'Now Jackie, concentrate. You can ride this bike out of this yard without hitting anything, stalling or falling off. Focus. Do it.' I opened the throttle the tiniest bit and crawled forward. Better slow and upright than quick and all over the place. I slowly rode out of the yard and round the corner and out onto the road. Mike crawled along behind me. We made our way through the traffic and out towards the city limits and then the houses and shops fell away and we were surrounded by fields. At last,the open road. I twisted the throttle and took off. Compared to my little Virago, cruising on this bike felt effortless as she swooped round the bends and raced across the straights. No plodding donkey this, more a slightly overweight race horse. I felt like yelling 'Yeee hiiiii' as I barrelled along. Maybe it's the Harley's American connection that made me feel all cowboy and horses, I don't know, but this was the sort of thrilling ride that I had been dreaming about. It was fantastic and when we pulled back into the dealer's yard I knew in my heart of hearts what my next bike was going to be. Mike came over, grinning from ear to ear. 'You seemed to be enjoying yourself on that one, what was it like?' Without even thinking about it I said 'It was wonderful, fantastic, I want one, I have to have one of those ..'' and we both started laughing. Mike was in full agreement. 'Now you're talking, let's go look at what they've got'. Obviously Mike had quickly realised that if I bought a Harley too there would be less chance of me moaning about him spending so much money on a V Rod. I didn't work that out till later as I was still riding high on the adrenalin from my test ride. So we went inside and I drooled over several Sportsters but in the end I decided to focus on selling my bike first and also seeing what was available second hand as I now knew that you pay top whack for bikes when you buy them through dealerships. I rode home singing 'You and me, we'll go motorbike riding in the sun and the wind and the rain' full of joy that my dreams were now finally taking shape.

Sensation on wheels

No matter what you ride, or what you may think of Harley-Davidson motorcycles, you have to respect a manufacturer that can create such icons of biking history...This bike [the V Rod] is the first of a new breed of motorcycle from the world's oldest manufacturer, and it's a motorcycle that taps into a hidden part of your emotions...it's mean, it's rebellious and ultra cool in one statement, and it goes like the wind..
Adrian Percival, Motorbikes Today, 2004

A couple of days later the Harley dealership rang to say Mike's bike was ready to collect. So I drove him over and dropped him off. I didn't wait because buying a Harley through a dealership is quite a performance. They go through all the paper work with you and then you have to have a video conference with the UK sales manager who welcomes you to the Harley brand and asks if you have had everything explained properly and if you are completely happy with your buying experience. I thought this was really weird but Mike was more fascinated by the technology and the fact that the video conferencing worked so well technically. Typical. He then rode the bike home. It was a lovely sunny day and the bike stood on the drive looking like a million dollars – which it should do when you think what it cost. I have to admit it did look stunning. Our neighbour, who is a mad biker and rides a suped up Suzuki Bandit 1200, came dashing over to take a look. 'Ha, you've bought a humpa-lumpa-dumpaloon then.' Pardon. We both just looked at him. 'What are you talking about?' I asked. Alex started laughing. 'Have you never heard of Wonder Warthog, the Hog of Steel. He was a character in a comic book back in the sixties.' I never cease to be amazed by the things that Alex knows about and is interested in. 'No, can't say I have. I don't remember seeing him in the Beano' I said. Alex snorted. 'I'm not talking about the Beano, I'm talking about real comics, underground comics. Surely you've heard of the Fabulous Furry Freak Brothers – they were done by the same guy.' I can never tell when Alex is being serious. Did he genuinely believe I would have read these comics or was he toying with me? Mike then piped up. 'Oh yes, I remember them.' Men, what a strange gender they are. Alex went on to explain that this Wonder Warthog character was used to take the mickey out of motor hobbyists and in one episode he has to buy a new motorbike so he rushes into shop and asks for the most expensive motorbike they have and is sold a Humpa-lumpa-Dumpaloon. I think the intention was that this translated as Humpalumpa = H = Harley and Dumpaloon = D = Davidson. So here was Mike with a very expensive Harley Davidson so obviously it was a Humpa – lumpa – Dumpaloon! We all just cracked up laughing.

Later that day I decided to do some research on the internet and sure enough there was information about it on the web. I emailed a man in America who claimed to have a huge collection of comics and asked him if he had heard of this character and knew of the episode concerned. He very kindly responded and sent me a picture of the actual scene where Wonder Warthog rushes into (and this is where Alex got it slightly wrong) a Heffalump – Dumpaloon dealership and asks the salesman 'What is the MOST EXPENSIVE motorcycle you have?' and the salesman, who is standing by a grossly over accessorised fat cruiser bike says 'That would be the new Heffalump – Dumpaloon 160 cubic inch radial four Sir! With accessories it comes to exactly $14,387.45!' It is really funny picture and I couldn't stop laughing as I showed it to Mike. He laughed too but not as loudly. I don't think he liked the idea of his wonderful new design icon being called a Heffalump Dumpaloon. Alex's only other comment on the bike was 'It's nice but it's not a real Harley is it? I mean real Harley's are quite agricultural looking and they're loud and bits fall off them.' So clearly Alex is one of those people who is not mesmerised by the Harley Davidson image.

Over the next few days we took both bikes out as often as possible. The long summer evenings were ideal for cruising around and we visited all our usual biking stops in the space of a few days. Mike's sister Kathryn took one look at the V Rod and jumped onto the saddle only to burn her leg on the hot exhaust. Our designer friend Les, like Mike, was wowed with the look of it and everywhere we went it attracted crowds of onlookers. Visits to the supermarket took ages as people came up and questioned Mike about the bike - what make was it, how long had he had it and how much did it cost? Fathers brought sons over to look at it, wives dragged husbands away from it, old men just stood staring at it. It was really strange. Mike found it all a bit disconcerting at first especially when they stood to watch him ride off and he felt very self conscious about his every move. How to look like a super experienced rider on a state of the art bike when you've only been riding a couple of years? My bike looked tiny at the side of it, talk about a Hog and a Hen. Still it was lovely to be out riding together again and Mike was obviously delighted with the V Rod. Now all we needed to do was get me a bigger bike.

Emotional rollercoaster

Some people believe holding on and hanging in there are signs of great strength. However, there are times when it takes much more strength to know when to let go and then do it.
Ann Landers

The day arrived when my advert appeared in the Bike Trader. It seemed odd to see my darling little bike described for all to see, in the hopes that someone would come and take her away from me. It made me feel a bit uneasy, like I was offering up one of my kids for adoption. If only I had enough money and garage space to keep her and buy another, but it was not to be. I did think about insisting on a home visit to anyone that wanted to buy her, like they do on animal rescue programmes. That way I could check out that she was going to live with an owner that would love and take care of her but I knew this was ridiculous and had to keep reminding myself 'It's only a motorbike'. Not long after the advert went into the magazine I noticed that I had two missed calls on my mobile phone. Why is it that when you want to hear your mobile phone you never can? Or perhaps it was some Freudian thing that because I didn't want to sell her I had somehow made myself deaf to ring tones. 'Oh dear, I bet I've lost a sale there' I thought to myself. I was trying to work out how to return the call when the phone rang again. It was a number I didn't recognise so I was quite hopeful that this was a possible buyer. In spite of this, it was with some trepidation that I answered the phone. 'I'm ringing about the bike – the one that's advertised in the Bike Trader." It was a male voice with a hint of Black Country accent. 'Yes'. I never realised that such a short word could be made to sound so suspicious. 'Well, I've tried to ring you a couple of times but nobody's answered, and well, I was just ringing up to see if you could you tell me a bit more about the bike please. I am looking for a small bike and yours look very nice.' He sounded friendly but it's hard to get a proper impression of someone over the phone. Mind you he had used the words 'very nice' when talking about my motorbike so that was a good sign and he was obviously being persistent about trying to get hold of me. 'What do you want to know?' Not very helpful, eh? Anyone would think I didn't want to sell this bike. 'Well, from your advert it sounds like a really lovely bike so I was just wondering – why are you selling it?' Hum. Really lovely bike. I liked the sound of this guy. 'Well, the thing is ..." and I explained to him my situation. We chatted on the phone for a few minutes and I have to say, I did like the sound of this potential buyer. It turned out he rode a scooter to work and was now wanting to progress onto a small motorbike and he thought mine looked ideal. He said he was definitely interested and, as he only lived about 20 miles away, he would come over the next evening to see it. When I put the phone down I couldn't believe it was that easy. The advert had only been in the magazine for about half a day and here I was with a potential buyer, and it didn't stop there. During the next three or four hours I had two more calls and I had to explain that I already had someone coming to see the bike. One man said he would ring again the next evening to see if I had sold it to the first enquirer so it looked like I wasn't going to have any problems making a sale.

The next night Les, the first caller, turned up. He was a really nice man. Friendly, down to earth and most importantly he obviously loved the bike the minute he saw her. 'Oh, you've kept that in nice condition, it's beautiful looking.' I stood there glowing with pride. The only problem was Les had never ridden a geared bike. He was used to twist and go scooters. 'Are these things hard to ride?' he asked. What do you say? No, not if you know what you are doing. It turned out he had done his basic training but then just used a scooter so had forgotten how to use gears. I spent the next five minutes explaining them to him and a further ten minutes helping him practice riding the bike up and down the drive. It was really strange watching someone struggle to get familiar with a bike that I now handled like a pro. Finally Les, with a big smile on his face, said 'Yes I want it but could you bring it over to me please 'cos I think I need to practice with it first. There's a big car park on an estate at the back of me and I think I'm going to go on there first with a mate of mine and get this gear thing sorted out, before I take it out on the road. So would that be okay, could you bring it over for me please?' What a sensible bloke. Just like me, he was going to practice on a car park first. Excellent. We agreed a price and a time on the following Saturday when I would drop the bike off. As he said goodbye and went off to his car with a

smile on his face, it was obvious Les was excited at the prospect
of owning this lovely bike. I said thanks and goodbye, went back
in the house, and felt gutted. Mike came home about half an hour
later from working late at the office. 'How did you get on?' he
asked. 'I sold it.' Mike turned to look at me. My tone of voice had
obviously let him know I was not overjoyed at the prospect.
'What are you so miserable about? You sold it. That's what you
wanted.' He was using his 'What are you like?' tone of voice.
'I know, but I love that bike, and if ..' I was whining pathetically.
Mike gave me a stern look. 'Oh shut up. This is ridiculous. You
need to move on. You said yourself you need a bigger bike now.
So stop thinking about the Virago and concentrate on sorting out
another bike for yourself. You're going to be without a bike by the
weekend so you need to focus on that now.' He was right. Now
he had the lovely new V Rod I needed to sort something out for
me. I got back on the Bike Trader website and started looking for
private sales of Harley Davidson Sportsters. I rang up a couple
but they had already gone and just as I was about to lose hope
I spotted an advert for a Harley Davidson Sportster Hugger. It
looked lovely in the photograph. The paint was a sort of greeny
blue, which I later learnt was a colour called something like Jade
Sapphire, and it came with lots of extras. A screen, saddle bags
and slash cut pipes whatever they are. It was in my price range
and about seventy miles away. 'What's a hugger?' I asked Mike.
'I've no idea, it must be a type of sportster. Look it up on the
internet' said Mike. Having already missed out on two bikes I
decided there wasn't time for that and the bike looked nice in the
picture so I rang the number. A woman answered, speaking with
a northern accent. Coming from Yorkshire and still having quite
a pronounced accent myself I instantly felt at ease. She asked
me to hold on whilst she went and got her husband. 'Hello there,

I understand you're interested in my bike.' It was the late Fred Dibnah or someone impersonating him. 'Yes, can you tell me a bit more about it please?' We chatted away for about ten minutes, at the end of which he knew all about my life as a would-be biker and I knew all about the bike. He had bought it from someone who hardly ever rode it but kept it in a garage and spent all his time adding accessories to it. Apparently this happens quite a lot with Harleys. People love the idea of owning one, so buy one, then dress them up in accessories but don't actually get round to riding them much. In our street, rumour has it that the bloke on the corner has a brand new sportster in his garage which he cleans every weekend but never rides! If I had known that then I might have approached him to see if we could do a deal. I ride the bike, he garages and cleans it! Anyway, Jim the seller, sounded trustworthy and friendly so I arranged to go and see the bike on the Saturday afternoon, after I had delivered the Virago to Les in the morning. It was all happening so fast. Mike, as usual, was right. By focussing on the new bike I was able to stop worrying about the old one. So everything was set for Saturday. This was going to be an exciting weekend. Little did I realise how exciting it was going to be as I gave my lovely bike a final, thorough cleaning.

Puncture stops sale

Everytime we say goodbye, I die a little,
Everytime we say goodbye, I wonder why a little...
Ella Fitzgerald

On the Saturday morning I awoke to clear blue skies and
sunshine. Perfect biking weather. After breakfast I got the bike
out of the garage and said an emotional goodbye to her. I knew
I had to do it then and not in front of Les, at the final hand over,
as I didn't want him to think he was dealing with a deranged
seller. Mike had agreed to follow me in the car. We still hadn't
insured the bikes to take pillion passengers so I couldn't come
home on the back of the V Rod. In any case the pillion seat on
the V Rod was more of a tiny point of leather, hardly big enough
for a small child's bottom never mind my more Rubenesque rear
end. There was no way I was going to perch on that, in spite of
Mike's repeated invitations. 'Go on, it will be fine, just hang on

to me.' Yeh, right. So we set off with me leading. As we headed out into open country between the two towns in my mind I started a conversation with the bike. 'You are going to love it with Les. He's a really nice bloke and think of it as a new adventure for you. He'll be taking you out every day, 'cos he is going to use to get to and from work. Now that'll be better than being stuck in a garage a lot of the time, won't it?' I've got to stop this talking to myself and inanimate objects, it's not good. Then, as we passed through one of the bigger villages I started to hear a funny noise, a sort of 'whumpa, whumpa, whumpa' noise. I looked around and up, thinking it might be a helicopter or something. No. Then I noticed that the bike wasn't handling very well, it was sort of lumpy on the road. I looked at the road surface thinking it's probably some peculiar new tarmac our council is trying out, but no, the road looked fine. Then, slowly it dawned on me that there was something wrong with the bike. What? I pulled up outside a children's nursery on the main road. I switched off the bike, kicked down the side stand and got off. Mike, who had pulled up behind me, sat looking at me through the windscreen, mouthing the word 'What?' at me. What? I didn't know what, the bike wasn't right. I quickly saw what the problem was, my back tyre was flat! I couldn't believe it. A flat tyre! How on earth had I got a flat tyre? I pulled off my helmet, turned towards Mike and mimed silent screaming. He jumped out of car and came over. 'What's the matter with you?' I pointed at the tyre. 'Oh, I see what you mean.' I could feel the onset of panic. 'How did that happen? How did I get a flat tyre like that?' I wailed. 'What do you mean, how did you get a flat tyre like that, you've obviously got a puncture. This has just happened, right? You were fine when we set off and it's not going to get suddenly that flat if it's just low on air, it's obviously a puncture.'

'A puncture? How did I get a puncture?' I shrieked. Mike just
looked at me and raised his eyes, obviously deciding that rational
conversation was not on the agenda at this moment in time.
Anything he might say was only going to make me worse, I
needed to calm down and absorb what was happening. I wasn't
quite ready for that and so spent the next few minutes moaning,
raging and, I hate to admit it, stamping my foot like a thwarted
child in the middle of a full blown tantrum. Mike held out his
hand. 'Give me your Roadside Assist card.' 'My what? What
are you on about?' 'Your Roadside Assist card, give it to me. We
need to get the bike sorted and they might be able to fix it here
or they'll have to tow it home.' Captain Sensible strikes again.
Yes, that was it, they could fix it and we would be on our way
again. I fished the card out of my pocket and rang them. They
took my details and said someone would be with me within the
hour. Within the hour? Oh this was really going to mess up my
timetable for the day. Mike said he was going to walk back down
into the village and buy a newspaper, having decided to wait
with me till the breakdown people turned up, and I sat on the
wall outside the day nursery and quietly panicked. I knew I had
to let Les know that I wasn't going to make the agreed time but
how to tell him that his newly awaited bike now had a puncture?
I took a deep breath and rang his number. 'Oh hi, is that Les?' I
tried to sound nonchalent. 'Yes, is that Jackie?' 'Yes, yes it is. Urr
look Les I've got a bit of bad news.' I tried to sound calm and
unruffled. 'What, has something happened? You haven't changed
your mind about selling it have you?' He sounded concerned.
'No, nothing like that. It's just that, well, I was bringing the bike
over to you and, well, I've had a puncture about half way across.'
I waited nervously for his reaction. 'Oh, that's a bit of bad luck.
What's happening now then?'

'Well, I've got the breakdown people coming out and they will either fix it here or tow me home and I will have to get it sorted. Sorry about this. If I can get it sorted, can I bring the bike over later today?' The line went quiet. 'Errm, well, no actually ..' I knew it, he was going to pull out of the sale. The whole thing was going to collapse. 'You see, we're going away camping this weekend, the weather being so good like, so we won't be around later. But we will be back tomorrow, about tea time so that would be okay.' Had I heard him correctly? 'Oh, so you still want the bike?' What am I like? 'Of course I want the bike, you can't help it if you get a puncture, that could happen to anyone. I'm just sorry that I can't be around later but I promised the missus I'd go camping this weekend ..' I felt a surge of relief. Of all the buyers, in all the towns, in all the world, he replied to my advert. How lucky was that? 'Yes, of course, that's fine. Look Les I'll ring you on your mobile when it's fixed and we can arrange another drop off time, is that okay?' 'Yes, that's fine. If I don't answer just leave a message and I'll ring you back. I'm not sure what sort of a signal there'll be around the campsite but I'll keep checking my phone. Well, I hope you get it sorted okay. Speak to you later. Bye.' What a nice man. I turned to the bike. 'He's a really nice man. You are going to be fine with him so you can stop all of this, punctures and stuff ..' I was speaking out loud and getting funny looks from passengers in cars going past. Whoops, must stop that.

Mike ambled back and offered me a Kit Kat. At times of crisis, eat chocolate. Just as I was finishing it off the breakdown van turned up with a special bike trailer attached to the tow bar. A friendly looking man got out and came over to me with a smile on his face. 'Well, it's a nice morning for it anyway ..' Funny isn't it, the different perspectives people have on situations. 'What have we got here then?' I pointed to the flat tyre. 'Oh dear, the back tyre is always more messy to deal with, got to get the gears and chain off and everything. Looks like a puncture. God job you stopped so quickly, no damage to the wheel rim, that'll fix up fine. Are you okay?' I gave a weak nod. I don't like to look like a damsel in distress in these situations but often feel a bit awestruck in the presence of highly practical people who sort out problems like this without batting an eyelid. 'So where do you want it taking?' I thought for a second and then said 'Home, I suppose.' My tone was borderline whining so I decided to say as little as possible. 'Where's home?' he asked. 'Back that way.' I nodded back down the road in the direction we had come. 'Okay, well let's get it on the trailer and then we can take it home for you. Is this going to be a job for you then, when you get back home?' He looked at Mike whilst he was saying this. Mike just grinned sheepishly. I couldn't believe it. By saying nothing he was going to let this guy think he could fix this puncture. Talk about macho posturing. Mike is quite practical, he can put up the odd shelf or two and has even laid a wooden floor in his time but repair a rear tyre puncture on a motorbike – I don't think so. 'He isn't going to fix it, he can't do things like that' I blurted out. A bit insensitive I know, but hey, I was under pressure. The bloke looked at Mike again with a sort of 'Is that right?' look on his face. 'Well, we haven't got anything to raise the back wheel off the floor with..' Mike mumbled. Raise the back wheel off the floor? Even if the bike was hanging from the rafters there was no way Mike was going to know how to remove all the gears and chain and everything. Who was he trying to kid? Before I could stop myself I blurted out 'Can't you just turn them over like bicycles?' Both men stared at me, with looks of disbelief on their faces, Mike's mechanical ineptitude completely forgotten in the face of my staggering ignorance. They turned towards each other and tried not to laugh out loud. 'What?' I said feeling my face start to turn red and hearing my internal voice start to shout JACKIE SHUT UP! 'No you can't, can you, turn them over I mean. Look, just ignore me, I'm not thinking straight. I'm supposed to be selling this bike to somebody in half an hour'. The breakdown bloke obviously took pity on me at this point and asked me about the proposed sale. I explained to him about my arrangements to sell this bike to Les in the morning and then to go look at the other bike in the afternoon. 'Look, why don't you let me take the bike to the Honda dealers back in town. They do work on all sorts of bikes, they're really good. I'm sure if you ask nicely they'll fix it for you, maybe even today. Back at the depot we all ride motorbikes and most of us use them when we get stuck with something so I know they're good. Why don't you give them a ring and see if they'll take the bike in and then we could tow it there?' Ha, fantastic, we were now back in the secret world of biking where everyone is a biker, loves bikes and is willing to help you out with yours. I couldn't believe my luck. So I rang the Honda dealers and, using my damsel in distress voice, I explained my situation, told them the breakdown man said they were brilliant and pleaded with them to help me. They were fantastic. 'Okay, bring it in and we'll take a look. If it is just a puncture we should be able to get that fixed for you.' I tried not to weep with gratitude.

With the bike safely strapped onto the trailer and Mike on his way home to put the kettle on and await my call to be picked up from the Honda dealers, I settled into the cab and began to calm down. I asked the breakdown man what sort of bike he had and he told me but I can't remember what he said it was. We started chatting about bikes and biking. He told me all about the other bikers in his depot and the sorts of bikes they rode and, when I explained that I was hoping to get a Harley Sportster he told me that one of the lads had just got a brand new one in the traditional orange and black colours and he was well pleased with it. He told me that he liked doing roadside assistance for bikes because bikers were such lovely people, really friendly and interesting. I was really enjoying this conversation. When I told him that I was a bit nervous about riding a bike with a bigger engine than the one I had got he said to me 'Don't worry. What I always say to people is, and don't take this wrong, with any bike it's all down to the throttle. You've got to treat your throttle like a woman.' He looked at me and smiled before continuing .. 'yeh, like a woman – wind her up slowly.' We looked at each other and then both burst out laughing. I made a mental note to tell Mike that one. When we arrived at the garage the mechanics were kindness itself and, after a quick look at the bike they said they would get it fixed by lunchtime. I was amazed and couldn't thank them enough. The breakdown man wished me luck and left just as Mike arrived to collect me. Ten minutes later I was back home having a cup of tea and mulling over the mornings events. Although I was relieved that I was getting my bike sorted I was still in a quandary about what to do about the visit to the Harley Sportster. Not having sold mine yet I didn't have the cash from that to use for any purchase I might make. In my mind, buying any new bike was dependent on selling the old one. Mike disagreed. 'Look, Les isn't going to pull out of your sale, he's made that clear. So you could still go see the sportster this afternoon and then sell your bike tomorrow.' Surely it wasn't that simple. 'But how am I going to do that when I haven't got the cash from my bike sale? I haven't got enough money to buy the sportster today.' Again Mike disagreed. 'That's just a cashflow problem. It's not that you haven't got the money, you just haven't got it now.' he said. 'Yes, so we agree I haven't got the money now ..' this was said in my schoolteacher to small child with learning difficulties voice. I hesitated and waited to see what Mike would come up with. 'Yes, so just borrow it and then pay it back when you make the sale'. Mike made this sound so obvious that I couldn't help but be intrigued. Did he have a bright idea up his sleeve? 'Okay, borrow it .. from where?' I was genuinely interested. 'Well, haven't you got an overdraft facility you could use?' he said, matter of factly. 'An overdraft facility? Are you mad, that would cost a fortune.' The schoolteacher tone was back. He persisted. 'Why, you would put the money back in on Monday.' I was not convinced, my Yorkshire upbringing has made me stubbornly resistant to spending money on things like interest charges. 'I know, but then they charge you bank charges for the rest of that month, or year or something ..'

Even though I was struggling with this idea of short term borrowing, my working class background having filled with me with dread at the thought of any sort of debt, my mind was beginning to process the idea. Where could I get my hands on some cash that I could repay quickly on Monday? I didn't want to lose this purchase if I could help it. You never know, the bike of my dreams could be waiting for me in Lancashire and all I needed to do was get my head around a cashflow problem. I raced around the house looking for savings pass books and bank statements. I demanded to know how much money Mike had in his personal account. We don't usually scrutinise each other's finances but this was an emergency. It took me about fifteen minutes to work out that by clearing out Mike's and my personal accounts and raiding our emergency savings I could just about scrap together enough money. So we raced into town to hit the banks before half day closing. With the money safely stowed in the bottom of my handbag we made our way home for a sandwich and to wait for the garage to ring about the bike. I had to collect that before we could leave for Lancashire because the Honda Dealerships is closed on Sundays and I wouldn't have a bike to sell if I didn't collect it today. Why is it that at times like these, time seems to speed up? I rang the insurers to check that if I did buy the sportster they would be able to insure me to ride it home. They said that would be fine but I would need to ring them before five o'clock as they then closed for the weekend. By now it was one o'clock in the afternoon and I could feel myself beginning to panic again. Once I collected the bike I needed to ride it home and garage it, then drive up to Lancashire, see the Sportster, make a decision and ring the insurers. How long would all that take? I was just mulling this over when my mobile phone rang. It was the garage to say the puncture was fixed. At last we could get moving. Mike dropped me off by the service entrance where my bike stood gleaming in the sun. I never realized that a fully inflated back tyre could look so good. I went inside to pay and thank everyone profusely. It turned out that the puncture was caused by a long metal pin, that had gone right through the tyre. They kept it and gave it to me saying they had never seen anything quite like it before and it had probably come off a tractor or something. Just my luck. They charged me £28 for a new inner tube and fitting which I thought was pretty good, especially when they had done it so quickly and at such short notice. I rode the bike home and garaged her then jumped into the car where Mike sat waiting patiently to start the long trek to Lancashire. Would this Harley Davidson Sportster, with all it's extras, be the bike of my dreams?

Bella joins the family

Just inside the door of this air-conditioned temple, a jaunty low-slung yellow bike sat coyly on her side stand perfuming the air with oil and polished leather. It was love at first sight. Roz hopped aboard before Scott, the dealer's son, had had time to check us out. She inspected the 'peanut' gas tank with it's bold '883 Sportster' insignia; caressed the stylish saddlebags designed for Poser's Boulevard, made to hold a half of nothing; wrapped her long hands around the sexy buckhorn handlebars; then frisked the leather tassels hanging demurely from various strategic sites waiting to stream bravely on the wind
Good Vibrations; Coast to coast by Harley. Tom Cunliffe

So the race was now on. Fortunately the M6 going north is reasonably quiet on a Saturday afternoon. We hurtled up the motorway, sweating in the afternoon sunshine that was now glaring in through the windscreen, and then followed Jim's directions to a neat looking little bungalow on a very steep hill on the outskirts of Burnley. The journey had taken us just under two hours and it was about four o'clock when we parked up and headed for the house, me thinking 'Whoa, this is going to be one hell of a hill start if I buy this one'. The front garden was neat and tidy, stocked with a nice selection of small annuals, all in flower. A good sign, this was obviously a house where people liked to keep things nice. The door was opened by a friendly looking lady who said 'Hello, are you the people to see Jim's bike?' There was that northern accent again. I don't know why but northern accents always make me feel comfortable. 'Yes, sorry we're late, we've had a heck of a day' I said. 'Oh well come in. I'll go shout Jim, he's up the garden. Would you like a cup of tea, you both look exhausted.' That's another thing, Northerners always offer you tea, not coffee or a soft drink, but tea. Lovely. We gratefully accepted the offer and went and sat in the living room. Again it was very clean, neat and tidy. Jim came in and if he wasn't related to Fred Dibnah he should have been. Same build, same smiley face, the only thing missing was the flat cap. 'Hello, ye' made it then, did you find us okay?' I instantly felt like I'd known him all of my life. 'Yes, the directions were fine, we just took it steady once we got off the motorway and apart from the last bit, where we got a bit mixed up and had to turn round, we were okay'. We English just love talking about the routes taken to get to places, directions followed and the state of the roads don't we? Whenever you go anywhere the first thing people ask you is 'Which way did you come then .. Oh, I never go that way ..Yes, that A road is a good road isn't it .. Oh I know I always avoid that junction myself ..' and so on. It's a national topic for discussion along with the weather. Before we could settle in to a long talk on this subject Mike piped up 'So can we see the bike then?'. He is really good at focusing on the task in hand unlike me, who is easily distracted. 'Oh yes, well you drink yer tea and I'll go get it out 'ut garage'. So we quickly drank up and then Jim's wife led us out through the back of the house to the drive. And there it stood. A gleaming vision of the archetypal Harley Davidson motorbike. The chrome was everywhere and polished to a mirror like sheen. The gleaming, bluish green paintwork, the studded leather saddle bags, the full American cop windscreen, sweep back Buck Horn handlebars, back rest and sissy bar and the 'Live to Ride, Ride to Live' eagle emblem on the battery casing all combined to dazzling effect. Wow! Motorbike for sale, only cowboys need apply. I was transfixed. Mike clearly was less impressed but nothing was going to compare to the V Rod for looks so that didn't bother me. He began to quiz Jim about the bike and the technical stuff that I could never understand. It turned out that Jim was a mechanic (more similarities with Fred Dibnah) and so he was able to wax lyrical about all things mechanical. He had obviously cared for this bike lovingly in the time that he had had it. It turned out he was only selling it because he had developed a heart condition and his doctor had told him to find a less exciting means of transport! Whilst Mike was checking out service history, stage one tuning and fuel consumption I was totting up the cost of all the accessories. I worked out that there was over a thousand pounds worth of 'extras' on the bike. Then I overheard Jim explaining to Mike that he still had the bike's original exhaust pipes and we should take them because when we came to sell the bike again we could pass them on the new owner too. This caught my attention. 'So what are these exhausts here then?' I asked as I looked at the exhaust pipes. To me, mechanical ignoramous that I am, an exhaust pipe is an exhaust pipe is an exhaust pipe.

'Those ert' slash pipes that go wi' stage 1 tuning. They're straight through pipes so they allow the air to move through the engine more smoothly. A lot of Harleys have these.' said Jim. 'Oh, is that a good thing then?' I asked. Jim gave me a slightly quizzical look. It was clearly dawning on him that he was selling his bike to someone who would barely register on the 'knows anything at all about mechanics' scale. I smiled. 'I'm sure they'll be fine' I smiled again. Jim was now looking very uncertain. 'Because they're straight through thez' no baffles as such so the bike is noisy. Look I'll turn the engine over so you can 'ear it.' He put the key in the ignition and started the bike up. The noise was unbelievable and both Mike and I instinctively jumped back. It was awesome, deafening, like someone was trying to land a Boeing 747 on Jim's drive. 'Ya' see, it's the real Harley sound' yelled Jim across the din. We just nodded, too dazed to say anything. 'It always sounds louder 'ere because we're between the houses, it's not quite this noisy once you get out on t' road'. Jim was looking at the bike with real pride in his eyes. He owned and rode a real Harley, who wouldn't look proud? He switched off the engine and silence fell. Mike and I just looked at each other, too stunned to say anything. Jim then told me to have a sit on the bike and see how it felt. I did and once again I experienced that thrilling feeling that comes from just sitting on a Harley. What is it about these bikes? Time was pressing on, if I was going to buy this bike I needed to ring the insurers. I trusted Jim and I needed a new bike as mine was being sold the next day. This looked like a good buy. Should I buy it? Should I leave it and do some more looking around? This was the first one I had come to see and perhaps there would be better deals elsewhere but it could take ages to track them down. Oh what to do? I turned to Mike who was standing there with a sort of bemused look on his face. 'Should I buy it then?' He chuckled as he said 'I don't know, you decide, you're going to ride it'. I took that as a good sign remembering the episode with the Virago when he had declared that we had others to see and ushered me away. He wasn't doing that here, so he must think it was okay. 'Okay, I'll buy it. How much do you want for it? Let's haggle.' I said, laughing. By now I felt very comfortable with Jim so didn't worry about saying something like that. We talked money and he agreed to knock some off mainly because the back tyre needed replacing. We shook on it and I raced into the house to phone the insurers. Jim's wife handed me a folder that had all the bike paperwork in it and after about ten minutes on the phone I was insured to ride the bike home. Phew, what a whirlwind. I felt all excited and giddy. Mike looked a bit shell shocked, everything had happened so quickly.

We began to get ready to go home. Mike took the spare pipes and the folder of paperwork and I got my biking gear out of the car. Jim talked us through the best way back to the motorway and then handed me the keys. I froze. This was it, I was going to ride a Harley, my Harley. I realised I was scared stiff. Jim looked concerned. 'You're gonna' be alright aren't you? You've ridden a big bike before haven't you?' He clearly needed reassuring on this point. 'Well, no, well yes I did my training on a bigger bike, it wasn't this big but it was bigger than the bike I ride ..' So, no reassurance there then. 'Are you going to be okay riding it home, I mean it's quite a long way isn't it?' He was now desperate for reassurance. Mike came over to see what the delay was. 'Are you ready? Shall we get off then?' Mike is wonderful, he always acts like I can do anything in any situation – except cook that is. 'Yes, I'm fine, I'm just a bit worried about this steep hill – you know getting off the drive and then facing up the hill. Why did you have to live on such a steep hill?' I tried to sound relaxed about the whole thing. 'Do you want me to get it off the drive and facing the right way up the hill?' said Jim. Before I could answer Mike said 'Do you want me to ride it home for you?' 'No, no I can do this. Jim can get it on the hill for me and then I can ride it home. Well, maybe not home, it is a long way. If I ride it to the first service station we could swop over and you could ride for a bit – sort of share the riding'. Mike smiled and agreed this was a good idea and would be a lot less tedious for him than driving all the way home. So whilst he went off to start the car, Jim rode the bike off the drive and onto the hill. I walked over and was about to put my helmet on when Jim said 'You 'av got earplugs haven't you?' Bringing earplugs hadn't even crossed my mind. 'No' I said. 'Well, you're going to need them, I suppose it'll be okay for now but when you get back you need to get yourself some earplugs'. I promised I would but thought that he was probably worrying too much and out on the open road the noise would be fine. Jim and his wife stood watching anxiously as I readied myself to do the biggest hill start of my life. Jim's wife came over at the last minute. I lifted my visor. 'Ring us when you get back to let us know you're okay. We won't be happy till we know you've got back okay'. She smiled nervously. Now I know what my eldest daughter Kathryn must have felt like when she started off on her two month backpacking adventure in Thailand, with the words 'Promise you will let me know you've arrived safely' ringing in her ears. I got on the bike. With a few final adjustments to my clothing I was ready for take off. To the theme tune of Thunderbirds, my internal voice kicked in. 'Right Jackie, hill start. Concentrate. Clutch in, first gear, foot brake on, few revs, open clutch, foot brake off and away we go …' I did it! I rode up the hill slowly but smoothly to the junction at the top. Stopped, then did my looking, then turned left onto the road Jim had told me to take and began my long trek home on my new Harley. The sun was beating down, it was a scorcher and as I rode along the M65 I felt like a San Fransisco cop, cruising on Ocean Drive. Yeeehiiiii. I felt so good, so clever for some reason. I had done it, I had bought myself a real Harley Davidson and I was riding it, on the motorway, in the sunshine. I kept looking in my rear mirrors to check Mike was following me, he was, and then giving him the thumbs up sign every time I successfully overtook a car. I felt amazing.

After about twenty minutes I began to settle down and start to really get a feel for the bike. The windscreen was very effective at cutting down the wind blast but I began to find that I had to duck my head slightly otherwise the top of it lined up perfectly with the middle of my eyes. Also it was beginning to get some squashed fly debris on it and I found myself inspecting the latest splattering rather than concentrating on the road. It felt a bit like sitting in a car behind a windscreen and I think I preferred looking at the open road with only the visual interference of a visor. The handlebars were at a slightly funny angle and this meant my arms were bent in such a way that I had to use my arm muscles to keep them in position. I would need to get them adjusted. However, these things were tiny niggles compared to the problem of the noise. The bike was deafening. Even out on the open road the noise was so loud it was like riding a mobile road drill. Jim was right, I definitely needed ear plugs! Signs for the first service station came into view and I wondered whether I should pull in and let Mike take over but I was enjoying myself too much to hand the bike over so I sailed past the exit and carried on. Mike, who had dropped back slightly, presumably expecting me to pull off at the services, slowly closed the gap between us over the next few miles. As we approached the Manchester Ship Canal bridge we entered roadworks and I had to slow right down. The noise of the bike attracted the attention of drivers and passengers in other vehicles. Some young lads on a coach took a real interest and I could see them pointing things out to each other as they discussed and admired the bike. I tried to look cool, like I had ridden across the states and back on this mean machine. Passengers in cars either nodded and smiled with a sort of 'nice one' gesture or scowled and looked at me as if to say 'bloody, noisy thing – who do you think you are?' Whatever the reaction it was certainly getting everyone's attention. The next service station came and went and the next. I just couldn't bring myself to pull off the road. I was enjoying this too much and just wanted to keep on riding. In the end I just rode the bike all the way home, pulling onto the drive after being 'in the saddle' for almost two hours. I was exhausted but ecstatic. No sooner had I pulled up and switched off the engine than Alex came walking over the road with his son Oscar in his arms. 'Now that's what I call a real Harley. I thought I could hear something coming from a while back, must have been this. Is it yours, have you bought it?' he asked as he scrutinised the bike. I dragged off my helmet, all smiles, and tried to act nonchalant. 'Yes, I've just been and bought it from a bloke in Burnley.' My voice sounded quiet and distant and I realised that I had gone a bit deaf from spending two hours sitting on top of a jack hammer. I had to concentrate to hear Alex. 'Burnley, eh? That's a bit of a trek. What, and you've ridden it back?' he looked at me quizzically. Alex was used to hearing me to go on about how lovely my little bike was and how nervous I was about getting a bigger one. 'Yes. I was supposed to stop and swop over with Mike but it was such fun that I just kept going'. I was laughing now, full of pride at my own daring.

'Nice one. Didn't I tell you that you'd soon get used to a bigger bike.' He gave me an admiring look before turning to inspect the bike yet again. I felt so pleased, Alex is hard to impress on the motorbiking front, him being such a seasoned and skilled biker, so his obvious admiration for my guts in just getting on the bike and riding it back made me feel justly proud. Then Mike pulled up and jumped out of the car. 'I thought you were going to stop and let me have a go?' He didn't look a happy man, which was not surprising when you think that he had just spent a beautiful warm and sunny Saturday afternoon driving about 200 miles on boring motorways. 'I'm sorry but I was enjoying myself so much I didn't want to stop.' I apologised. 'It was fantastic but the only trouble is that I've gone deaf now. This bike is really noisy'. Alex grinned. 'Yes, but that's half the charm. It's a real Harley and that is how they are supposed to sound – loud and proud!' 'Well it's certainly loud' I added as I started to unzip my biking jacket. 'I must just go and ring Jim and his wife and let them know I got back okay' and I left the two men and boy to discuss the bike and it's relative merits. Once in the house I started to try and remove my biking gear and realised that I had sweat so much in the heat that I was soaked inside and the clothing was all stuck to me. It took me a good five minutes to peel off my soaking jacket and trousers. In fact, when I weighed myself the next morning I found that I had lost 3lbs on that momentus journey. Talk about a mobile sauna. I quickly rang Jim and he sounded relieved that I had made it okay. I also told him I was now deaf and he did say he had warned me and I must go and get ear plugs first thing if I didn't want to damage my ears.

Back out on the drive the men had been joined by Alex's partner Lyndsey. She was well impressed with my efforts. 'What you just got on it and rode it a 100 miles home?' 'Yep.' I said proudly, I was now basking in glory. Lindsey looked wistful. 'I love Harleys. I used to go out with a bloke who had a Harley. They're so full of character. I can't believe you've bought one.' Lyndsey is also a biker but she rode a little Honda 125. She had passed her test for a bigger bike a few years back and had then ridden a bike like Mike's first Honda but she never felt very happy on it and had dropped it a few times. When she was pregnant with Oscar she packed in riding and, as a result, she had lost her confidence. Now that Oscar was a bit older she was trying to get her confidence back by just riding a small bike again. We all studied the bike and Oscar, who loves all things transport, had a sit on it. A full appraisal now completed Alex stepped away from the bike. 'I'm not so keen on all this Live to Ride, Ride to Live stuff on the mirrors and battery case, and I've never really been one for screens, I prefer my bikes to be naked'. He was now grinning. I had to agree with him now that I was over the initial excitement of buying a Harley. We chatted a bit more, my hearing still not working properly and then Alex, Lyndsey and Oscar said their goodbyes and we went in for a drink. As we slumped on the couch with our cups of teas I felt exhausted but full of pride. I had done it, I had bought a Harley and ridden it home, amazing. The only problem now was how to garage it as the garage would not hold three bikes. In the end I decided to garage the Harley and store my little bike on the drive under a cover. That would have to do for now but it was imperative that I try to get the Virago to Les the next day.

Goodbye baby cruiser

*The pebbles forgive me, the trees forgive me, So why can't you
forgive me?*
I don't see what anyone can see, in anyone else, but you.
The Moldy Peaches

The next morning the skies were grey and overcast and the wind
was up. I wanted to get the bike out but eventually common
sense prevailed and I decided against it. Riding in the wind is no
picnic. Instead we drove into Birmingham to have a potter around
the bookshops. We only really go into Birmingham on a Sunday
when it is relatively quiet and easy to wander around. Words like
crowds and shopping in the same sentence are guaranteed to keep
us at home. On the way back it started raining and I watched,
with real admiration, all the bikers doggedly weaving through the
thick traffic, bikes loaded down with every kind of pannier and
bag and many with pillion passengers, as they pressed north on

the motorway system. Motorway riding is no fun but unavoidable when you want to cover long distances to your preferred biking destination. For example, many bikers like to go to Scotland for biking holidays so they have to make the long trek north just to get started.

After lunch the sky started to clear and I tried to ring Les on his mobile phone to sort out dropping off the Virago. I got his answerphone so I left a message asking him to ring me when he got back. A couple of hours later when I was doing some gardening, which always takes my mind off things and helps me to relax, Mike came out of the house with my mobile in his hand. 'It's Les, for you'. I brushed the dirt off my hands and took the phone. 'Hi Les.' 'Hi Jackie. I got your message. We're on our way home now so if you want to bring the bike over we should be back in about an hour.' My beloved buyer. 'Okay. Do you want me to bring it then or wait a bit till you get settled back in?' 'No, just bring it over when you're ready, that's okay with us'. 'Okay, see you in about an hour, an hour and a half'. 'Okay, see you then". Again I thanked my lucky stars for getting Les as my buyer. I went and told Mike about the proposed drop off time. 'Oh, so I suppose you'll want me to follow in the car again'. He didn't look thrilled at the prospect which was understandable after the long motorway haul the day before. 'Yes please. This will be the last time though because then the bikes will all be sorted.' I tried to look incredibly grateful. He mumbled something like 'It had better be' and wandered off to finish whatever he was doing. As it turned out, we took an hour to get ready to go. Mike was making home made ice cream and we had to wait for the machine to finish. I uncovered the bike and gave it a quick wipe over and then got into my gear for the journey to Les's house. As Mike pulled the front door shut and headed for the car he called to me 'Okay, lets get moving, we need to get rid of this bike and get back.' He obviously had other important culinary tasks to attend to and this was nothing more than an irritating interruption. I froze and, for a moment, just wished the motorbike had ears so that I could put my hands over them. Was he mad? I didn't want the bike hearing things like 'We need to get rid of this bike'. Who knows what might happen, another puncture perhaps? I couldn't stop myself from thinking that the bike had feelings and would know something was afoot and decided not to go along with it. 'Shhhhhh…' I called to him. 'What?' I pointed down at the bike and wagged my finger in the classic 'Don't say anything in front of the bike' gesture. Mike just shook his head and rolled his eyes as in the classic 'What is she like?' gesture, then got in the car and waited for me to lead the way. I knew the main road that Les's street ran into so was planning on getting to the main road and then turning up past the pub he had told me about and into his street. In my mind I began a conversation with the bike, a bit like people talk to horses as they guide them out on to the race course. 'Okay, well isn't this nice. The skies have cleared up and we are going for a little ride. Guess what, we are going back to the Harley garage. Yes, that's it, that is why Mike is driving you see. He is going to test ride another motorbike and we are going to accompany him. Won't that be nice. You know you like doing that, so no silly punctures or breakdowns today eh?' I felt anxious after yesterdays attempt had failed so dramatically. We rode on. As we approached the town I began to work my way around towards the main road I knew, only to find it was completely closed off due to roadworks. Damn. Why was everything conspiring to make it so hard for me to hand over this bike? I followed the diversion signs but knew from our first test ride on the V Rod that these had been put out by someone who enjoyed sending the traffic round in circles and up blind alleys. Oh joy. After about ten minutes riding around I pulled over to ask a man with a small dog for directions. Not a good idea. The dog starting barking wildly as the man neared the bike so he yanked his lead hard and, clearly avoiding all eye contact, marched on down the street. Great. Mike, who had pulled up, came over. 'I thought you knew the way to this bloke's house.' 'I do, did, but the road works won't let you go down the Penn Road.' Mike was looking decidedly fed up, which made me feel even more stressed because he has a history of just packing up when he gets fed up with something. All I needed now was for him to abandon me and head off home. 'Look, wait a bit, it's near here I know it is, I just need to ask someone for directions.' I looked around frantically and, as per usual, just when you need someone to ask there was no one in sight. Just as I resigned myself to finding a garage or shop where I could ask, an older man with a teenage boy walked around the corner and started looking at the bike. So, they were interested in bikes, good, they might be less wary of approaching a biker. I pulled up my visor and yelled as loud as I could 'EXCUSE ME ..' They looked at me and came over. Over the sound of the engine I asked them directions and they, bless them, gave me simple, easy to follow directions. I thanked them and set off again, thinking I wouldn't be able to do that on the Harley, at least not without a megaphone. At last, we pulled up outside Les's house and before I could get off the bike he and his wife and another couple were out of the house admiring it. And I have to admit it did look lovely, all gleaning and clean. I felt very proud standing there about to hand over what was obviously a much loved and cared for bike. Les's wife just stood there looking and then said 'Oh it's a nice looking bike Les' and then she and the couple stood chatting and casting admiring glances in our direction whilst I rang Les through the controls once again. Then we went inside and I was pleased to see that the house was really lovely, minimal decoration, tastefully done and very, very clean and tidy. I knew then that my bike had come to a really good home and I felt happy, really for the first time, about selling it. We sorted out all the documents, handed over keys and money and we said our goodbyes. As we drove off I looked back at the bike and called out 'You'll be fine with Les, trust me, he will look after you, you'll have a great time'.

Mike looked at me, shook his head and said 'What are you like?' but I didn't care. I loved that bike and that bike loved me and this was the end of a beautiful relationship but it was time to move on and my big noisy Harley was waiting for me at home.

Living with 2 Harleys

...whatever you do in your life that you think is important, leave it, borrow or steal the money, and take the trip. Do it now. Stop reading, go out and buy a Harley, and get the hell out before the hot breath you smell on your neck becomes teeth and your life kills you.'
Zero to Sixty: The motorcycle journey of a lifetime. Gary Paulsen

So there I was, the proud owner of a Harley Davidson Sportster Hugger 883 motorbike. Although described in the magazines as the baby of the Harley Davidson line up and an 'entry level' Sportster, the bike felt big and powerful to me. Every time I got it out of the garage I felt a nervous thrill run down my spine. I often had to get Mike to help me to manoeuvre it around because, with the bike weighing around 220kg and me weighing around 66kg, it was very heavy and unwieldy especially compared to the little Virago, but I was undaunted. In fact, following one unfortunate incident where I dropped the bike because I didn't have the strength to hold it, I joined a weekly weight training class to try and build up some muscle, especially in my arms. I also began to wear ear plugs regularly after reading an article which pointed out the damage that could be done by spending long hours in the company of very noisy motorbikes. It was whilst visiting my sister in law Kathryn and complaining of not being able to hear what she was saying that she promptly produced some foam ear plugs and insisted that I wear them. She wore them to help her sleep through the day when she was working night shifts. With the ear plugs in place, the journey home was a whole new experience. They were so effective at muffling the normally loud booming sound of the engine that it felt a bit like riding underwater with a divers helmet on. From then on I always tried to remember to put in my ear plugs and although these made riding much more bearable they did sometimes hurt my ears, especially on long journeys. Sometimes I would set off and realise that I had forgotten to put them in so would have to stop and remove my helmet and gloves, get the ear plugs out of my jacket pocket, put the ear plugs in and then get the helmet and gloves back on. It was such a fiddle and, as a result, I often suffered the outward journey unplugged rather than make all the effort to put them in. I soon realised that I had to find another way to solve the noise problem and I did eventually by having the original, quieter exhaust pipes put back on, much to the disgust of the mechanics at the Harley garage who said it didn't sound like a proper Harley anymore! Maybe not, but it was a whole lot more pleasant to ride. The most surprising thing though was how quickly I forgot my little bike as I struggled to get to grips with this new one. Where the Virago has been a little sweetie pie of a bike, this thing was a real hand full and I quickly named her Bella. Why? I was watching a programme on TV about the explorer Benedict Allen and he was travelling across some deserts with three camels, the leading one of which was a really cantankerous old boy named Nelson. He had to be coaxed along, bullied, threatened, stroked and cajoled to do what Benedict wanted him to do and it suddenly struck me that Bella was exactly the same albeit mechanical. She was a struggle to get out of the garage, she bellowed so loudly when I started her up that everyone within half a mile could hear her antisocial racket and this usually brought Alex, Lyndsey and Oscar to their gate to watch the start up performance as I coaxed her off the drive. Once she was out on the road, some days she would be really good and cruise around the place happily but other days, maybe if the weather was a bit colder or the traffic more slow moving, she would splutter and cough loudly just like a camel spitting and barking and she had to be coaxed along with a firm hand. She had so much character and reminded me of some of the old cars that I had owned in my time, where unless you followed specific rituals and routines they wouldn't start or kept stalling or generally just lost the will to make progress unless they were lovingly nursed along. I even, on occasions, found myself yelling at her 'BELLA, STOP IT, SETTLE DOWN, BEHAVE YOURSELF' because some days she just seemed to have got out of the wrong side of the garage if you see what I mean. It wasn't long before I removed the windscreen, changed the mirrors to ones with longer stems that I could actually see out of, adjusted the Buck Horn handlebars to a slightly more comfortable position and had a new back tyre. Bella soon began to feel like I had owned and ridden her all my life. I could now keep up with Mike everywhere except on the motorway where the V Rod just took off into the distance. I found that a steady 60 mile an hour felt fine but much above that and the bike began to vibrate all the way up through the footpegs, my feet, my legs and into my bottom. Mike thought this was hilarious and began to call her my Sporting Tractor! I could reach higher speeds if I needed to but long journeys without a windscreen and at bone shaking high speeds always left me feeling like I had been beaten all over with sticks so I preferred to look for slower, more scenic routes. Riding through the dales, shattering the peace and scaring the wildlife, I began to realise that it took real skill to ride Bella well. I couldn't always rely on the extra power to get me out of trouble. Riding at the higher speeds I had to learn to read the road more quickly and give more forethought to gear changes. Mike, on the other hand, seemed to get away with using practically any gear in almost any situation as his bike had so much readily available power. I also began to feel more in charge of the bike with a sort of 'I'll decide where we'll go and how fast' approach rather than 'Oh look where this bike is taking me'. I began to grow up as a biker on Bella and I loved her with all her funny ways, which is why I now find it hard to believe that I only had her for a year before trading her in for an even bigger Harley but that's another story. Around the time that I was getting to grips with Bella the BBC conducted a survey on something like 50 things to do before you die and Mike showed me an article in the paper which had people rating 'riding a motorbike on the open road' somewhere in the 20's. I looked it up on their website and there it was at number 24 in the list of the top 50 things to do before you die:

24: Riding a Harley Davidson, anywhere you fancy ..

Further down the page I read 'For many enthusiasts, a Harley-Davidson is not just a motorcycle. It's an icon, a slap in the face of mainstream sensibilities, a fantasy, a declaration of freedom, a way of life, even a religion..' and I had to smile. So all over the country there were thousands of people who wanted to ride a Harley Davidson. Thousands of people who knew deep down what a great experience it would be. And me, well I was lucky enough to have one in the garage and could get it out and ride it whenever the mood took me. It brought a lump to my throat and I felt humbled. I had been very lucky and life had been very good to me. I had a wonderful family and a grandson on the way, a thriving business, a beautiful home and a partner for life in Mike. I also had a Harley Davidson motorbike. What more could a person ask for? Well, a bigger bike actually but that really is another story.

www.ingramcontent.com/pod-product-compliance
Lightning Source LLC
Chambersburg PA
CBHW021048090426
42738CB00006B/237